NATIONAL NANOTECHNOLOGY INITIATIVE

STRATEGIC PLAN

National Science and Technology Council

Committee on Technology

Subcommittee on Nanoscale Science,
Engineering, and Technology

February 2014

National Science and Technology Council
Committee on Technology (CoT)
Subcommittee on Nanoscale Science, Engineering, and Technology (NSET)

CoT Chair: **Thomas Kalil,** Office of Science and Technology Policy
CoT Executive Secretary: **Randy Paris,** Office of Science and Technology Policy

NSET Subcommittee Chair:
Altaf H. Carim, Office of Science and Technology Policy

National Nanotechnology Coordination Office:
Lloyd J. Whitman, Interim Director

NSET Subcommittee Executive Secretary:
Tarek R. Fadel, National Nanotechnology Coordination Office

NSET Subcommittee Participants

Office of Science and Technology Policy (OSTP)
Altaf H. Carim*

Office of Management and Budget (OMB)
Danielle Jones*
James Kim*
Celinda Marsh*

Consumer Product Safety Commission (CPSC)†
Mary Ann Danello*
Treye A. Thomas*

Department of Commerce (DOC)

Bureau of Industry and Security (BIS)
Kelly Gardner*

Economic Development Administration (EDA)
Thomas Guevara*

National Institute of Standards and Technology (NIST)
Heather Evans*
Ajit Jillavenkatesa*
Debra L. Kaiser

U.S. Patent and Trademark Office (USPTO)
Gladys Corcoran*
David R. Gerk*
Bruce Kisliuk*

Department of Defense (DOD)
Mostafiz Chowdhury
Jeffrey DePriest*
Akbar Khan*
Heather Meeks
Brian D. Pate
Gernot S. Pomrenke*
Lewis E. Sloter*
David M. Stepp*
Peter Vandeventer

Department of Education (DOEd)
Peirce Hammond*

Department of Energy (DOE)
Harriet Kung*
George Maracas*
John C. Miller*
Andrew R. Schwartz*
Brian G. Valentine*

Department of Health and Human Services (DHHS)

Agency for Toxic Substances and Disease Registry (ATSDR)
Candis M. Hunter

Food and Drug Administration (FDA)
Jed Costanza*

National Institute for Occupational Safety and Health (NIOSH)
Charles L. Geraci*
Vladimir V. Murashov*

National Institutes of Health (NIH)
Piotr Grodzinski*
Lori Henderson*

Department of Homeland Security (DHS)
Eric J. Houser*
Richard T. Lareau*

Department of the Interior (DOI)

U.S. Geological Survey (USGS)
Sarah Gerould*

Department of Justice (DOJ)

National Institute of Justice (NIJ)
Joseph Heaps*

Department of Labor (DOL)

Occupational Safety and Health Administration (OSHA)
Janet Carter*

Department of State (DOS)
Christopher M. Cannizzaro*
Ken Hodgkins*

Department of Transportation (DOT)
Peter Chipman*
Jonathan R. Porter*

Department of the Treasury (DOTreas)
John F. Bobalek*

NSET Subcommittee Participants (continued)

Environmental Protection Agency (EPA)
Tina Bahadori*
William K. Boyes*
Nora F. Savage*
Philip G. Sayre*

Intelligence Community (IC)

Office of the Director of National Intelligence (ODNI)
Richard Ridgley*

National Reconnaissance Office (NRO)
Matthew Cobert*

National Aeronautics and Space Administration (NASA)
Michael A. Meador*

National Science Foundation (NSF)
Parag R. Chitnis*
Khershed Cooper*
Barbara Karn
Fred Kronz
Thomas P. Rieker*
Mihail C. Roco*
Grace J. Wang*

Nuclear Regulatory Commission (NRC)†
Brian Thomas*

U.S. Department of Agriculture (USDA)

Agricultural Research Service (ARS)
Robert Fireovid*

Forest Service (FS)
World L.-S. Nieh*
Theodore H. Wegner*

National Institute of Food and Agriculture (NIFA)
Hongda Chen*

U.S. International Trade Commission (USITC)†
Elizabeth R. Nesbitt*

Acknowledgments

The individuals listed below dedicated considerable time and expertise to write and produce the *2014 NNI Strategic Plan*.

Strategic Planning Co-Chairs: Debra L. Kaiser (NIST) and World L.-S. Nieh (USDA/FS)

Strategic Planning Project Manager: Stacey Standridge (NNCO, contractor)

Writing Team Section Chairs and Co-Chairs: Lisa Friedersdorf (Nanotechnology Signature Initiative Chair, NNCO, contractor), Charles L. Geraci (Goal 4 Co-Chair, DHHS/NIOSH), Fred Kronz (Goal 4 Co-Chair, NSF), Michael A. Meador (Goal 2 Chair, NASA), Brian D. Pate (Goal 1 Co-Chair, DOD), Robert G. Rudnitsky (Goal 3 Chair, NIST), Lewis E. Sloter (PCA Chair, DOD), and David M. Stepp (Goal 1 Co-Chair, DOD)

Additional Writing Team Contributors: John F. Bobalek (DOTreas), Christopher M. Cannizzaro (DOS), Altaf H. Carim (OSTP), Janet Carter (DOL/OSHA), Khershed Cooper (NSF), Cheryl David-Fordyce (NNCO, contractor), Meredith M. Drosback (OSTP, AAAS S&T Policy Fellow), Heather Evans (NIST), William Frazier (DOD), J. Aura Gimm (DOD, AAAS S&T Policy Fellow), Lori Henderson (DHHS/NIH), Geoffrey M. Holdridge (NNCO, contractor), Candis Hunter (DHHS/ATSDR), Alan J. Hurd (DOS, Franklin Fellow), Saber Hussain (DOD), Ajit Jillavenkatesa (NIST), Barbara Karn (NSF), Igor Linkov (DOD), Heather Meeks (DOD), John C. Miller (DOE), Vladimir V. Murashov (DHHS/NIOSH), Sri Nadadur (DHHS/NIH), Elizabeth R. Nesbitt (USITC), Carlos L. Peña (DHHS/FDA), Robert Pohanka (NNCO), Dennis L. Polla (DOD), Thomas P. Rieker (NSF), Andrew R. Schwartz (DOE), Calvin Shipbaugh (DOD), Treye A. Thomas (CPSC), Brian G. Valentine (DOE), Peter Vandeventer (DOD), Christopher Weis (DHHS/NIH), Lloyd J. Whitman (NIST), and Steven Zullo (DHHS/NIH)

February 26, 2014

Dear Members of Congress:

Nanotechnology—the science of the very small—is a relatively young field, ripe for new discoveries and understanding. But nanotechnology is already changing the world. Advances enabled by Federal investments in nanotechnology underpin a wide variety of applications and products on the market today, including electronic circuitry, displays, sensors, battery technology, disease therapeutics, and wear-resistant coatings.

Since 2001, the National Nanotechnology Initiative (NNI) has served as the vehicle for coordinating and reporting on activities in this dynamic field across the Federal Government. Twenty departments, independent agencies, and independent commissions participate in the NNI, representing a wide variety of missions, responsibilities, interests, and expertise. The NNI Strategic Plan outlines the broad goals of the Initiative and supports those goals by delineating specific objectives. It provides a framework to foster coordination and collaboration across agencies and serves as a guide for individual NNI member agencies as they prioritize activities relating to research, development, training, and infrastructure.

The NNI has evolved over time in both its structure and its emphasis. In recent years there has been growing activity in environmental, health, and safety research; cooperation among regulatory agencies; and commercialization and advanced manufacturing at the nanoscale. These shifts and others are reflected in the 2014 Strategic Plan, which describes a revised reporting structure for Program Component Areas; details a number of focused, topical Signature Initiatives; summarizes the roles of the National Science and Technology Council's Subcommittee on Nanoscale Science, Engineering, and Technology and related bodies; and discusses the growing array of intersections with related Federal initiatives.

Great progress has been made in the past thirteen years, but much more remains to be discovered. The NNI Strategic Plan will help ensure that America remains a global leader in nanotechnology while this fast-maturing discipline continues to support economic growth, job creation, and solutions to a range of national challenges.

Sincerely,

John P. Holdren
Assistant to the President for Science and Technology
Director, Office of Science and Technology Policy

Table of Contents

Tables

The NNI

The National Nanotechnology Initiative (NNI) is the U.S. Federal Government's interagency activity[1] for coordinating research and development (R&D) as well as enhancing communication and collaborative activities in nanoscale science, engineering, and technology. This chapter describes the NNI, the vision and goals that frame the NNI, and the related interests and activities of the participating NNI agencies.[2]

Introduction

Nanotechnology is the understanding and control of matter at dimensions between approximately 1 and 100 nanometers, where unique phenomena enable novel applications. Work within the intersecting disciplines at the core of nanotechnology innovation—including physical, life, and social sciences and engineering—has revealed the potential of engineered nanomaterials (ENMs) and nanoscale processes to collect and store energy, reinforce materials, sense contaminants, enable life-saving drugs, and shrink and accelerate computational devices in both incremental and paradigm-shifting ways. Further, nanotechnology has enabled development of entirely new materials and devices that can be exploited in each of these and countless other applications.

The United States has set the pace for nanotechnology innovation worldwide with the **National Nanotechnology Initiative (NNI)**. Launched in 2001 with eight agencies participating, the NNI today consists of the individual and cooperative nanotechnology-related activities of 20 Federal departments and independent agencies with a range of research and regulatory roles and responsibilities (see Table 1). Eleven of the participating agencies have R&D budgets that relate to

What is Nanotechnology?*

Nanotechnology is the understanding and control of matter at dimensions between approximately 1 and 100 nanometers (nm), where unique phenomena enable novel applications. Encompassing nanoscale science, engineering, and technology, nanotechnology involves imaging, measuring, modeling, and manipulating matter at this length scale.

A nanometer is one-billionth of a meter. A sheet of paper is about 100,000 nanometers thick; a single gold atom is about a third of a nanometer in diameter. Dimensions between approximately 1 and 100 nm are known as the nanoscale. Unusual physical, chemical, and biological properties can emerge in materials at the nanoscale. These properties may differ in important ways from the properties of bulk materials and single atoms or molecules.

x 100,000

x 100,000

Single-walled Carbon Nanotube
1 nanometer diameter

Strand of Hair
100 micrometers diameter

House
10 meters wide

* The scope of this definition was established by the NNI at its inception for identifying and coordinating Federal nanotechnology research and development as well as for facilitating communication.

---

[1] The 21st Century Nanotechnology Research and Development Act refers to the NNI as a "program." To avoid confusion with agency-specific definitions of the word "program," the NNI will hereafter be referred to as the "Initiative."

[2] Participants in the NNI include Federal departments, independent agencies, and independent commissions, which are collectively referred to as participating "agencies" within this document.

nanotechnology, with the reported NNI budget representing the collective sum of these investments. Funding support for nanotechnology R&D stems directly from NNI agencies, not from any centralized NNI budget. As an interagency effort, the NNI informs and influences the Federal budget and planning processes through its participating agencies and through the National Science and Technology Council (NSTC).

Coordinated under the Nanoscale Science, Engineering, and Technology (NSET) Subcommittee of the NSTC's Committee on Technology (CoT), the NNI provides a framework for a comprehensive nanotechnology R&D program by establishing shared goals, priorities, and strategies that complement agency-specific missions and activities and that provide avenues for individual agencies to leverage the resources of all participating agencies. Further, the NNI provides a central interface for stakeholders and interested members of the general public, including those from academia, industry, regional/state organizations, and international counterparts. To these ends, the National Nanotechnology Coordination Office (NNCO) provides technical and administrative support to the NSET Subcommittee, serves as a central point of contact for Federal nanotechnology R&D activities, and provides public outreach on behalf of the NNI. Working groups established by the NSET Subcommittee provide an infrastructure to strengthen interagency coordination and collaboration on critical nanotechnology issues, and coordinators are named in specific cross-cutting areas to serve as primary points of contact for these topics.

U.S. leadership in fundamental nanotechnology R&D under the NNI has established a thriving nanotechnology R&D environment, laid the crucial groundwork for developing commercial applications and scaling up production, and created demand for many nanotechnology and manufacturing jobs in the near term. The NNI has dramatically expanded scientific understanding of nanoscale phenomena and has enabled development and engineering for a variety of applications through an extensive and unparalleled infrastructure of R&D centers, networks, and user facilities. The Federal investments in nanotechnology R&D have positioned the United States to address key national priorities, bring new expertise to bear on important scientific and social problems, strengthen the social contract between science and society, and inspire a growing number of students to pursue careers in science, technology, engineering, and mathematics. Growing from the NNI agencies' ongoing investments in foundational R&D, NNI activities aimed at accelerating commercialization have taken on added importance.

While the progress of nanotechnology innovations to date has been significant, numerous challenges still exist, and the tremendous potential anticipated from nanoscale R&D is still far from total realization. Achieving the full value of nanotechnology innovation depends on sustained foundational R&D and on focused commercialization efforts. Barriers need to be lowered and pathways streamlined to transfer emerging nanotechnologies into economically viable applications. Researchers, educators, and technicians with new, cross-cutting skills are also required. Furthermore, there must be a national commitment to responsibly develop nanotechnology with balanced and transparent consideration of the benefits and risks associated with particular ENMs in specific applications. For these reasons,

Table 1: Federal Departments and Agencies Participating in the NNI

11 Federal departments and independent agencies and commissions with nanotechnology R&D budgets

Consumer Product Safety Commission (CPSC)[†]

Department of Commerce (DOC)

    National Institute of Standards and Technology (NIST)

Department of Defense (DOD)

Department of Energy (DOE)

Department of Health and Human Services (DHHS)

    Food and Drug Administration (FDA)

    National Institute for Occupational Safety and Health (NIOSH)

    National Institutes of Health (NIH)

Department of Homeland Security (DHS)

Department of Transportation (DOT)

    Federal Highway Administration (FHWA)

Environmental Protection Agency (EPA)

National Aeronautics and Space Administration (NASA)

National Science Foundation (NSF)

U.S. Department of Agriculture (USDA)

    Agricultural Research Service (ARS)

    Forest Service (FS)

    National Institute of Food and Agriculture (NIFA)

9 other participating departments and independent agencies and commissions

Department of Education (DOEd)

Department of the Interior (DOI)

    U.S. Geological Survey (USGS)

Department of Justice (DOJ)

    National Institute of Justice (NIJ)

Department of Labor (DOL)

    Occupational Safety and Health Administration (OSHA)

Department of State (DOS)

Department of the Treasury (DOTreas)

Intelligence Community (IC)

    Office of the Director of National Intelligence (ODNI)

Nuclear Regulatory Commission (NRC)[†]

U.S. International Trade Commission (USITC)[†]

Also participating from the Department of Commerce (DOC), listed above

    Bureau of Industry and Security (BIS)

    Economic Development Administration (EDA)

    U.S. Patent and Trademark Office (USPTO)

KEY [†] Denotes an independent commission that is represented on NSET but is non-voting broad-based coordination and integration of development efforts across Government agencies, academic disciplines, industries, and countries remain critical to attaining the full economic and societal benefits promised by nanotechnology.

The **National Nanotechnology Initiative Strategic Plan** is the framework that underpins the nanotechnology work of the NNI agencies. It aims to ensure that advancements in and applications of nanotechnology continue in this vital area of R&D, while addressing potential concerns about future and existing applications. Its purpose is to facilitate achievement of the NNI vision and goals, which are outlined below, by laying out guidance for agency leaders, program managers, and the research community regarding planning and implementation of nanotechnology R&D investments and activities.

The NSET Subcommittee solicited multiple streams of input to inform the development of this revised NNI Strategic Plan. Independent reviews of the NNI by the President's Council of Advisors on Science and Technology and the National Research Council of the National Academies—strongly supportive of the NNI overall—have made specific recommendations for improving the Initiative.[3] Additional input came from the *2013 NNI Strategic Planning Stakeholder Workshop* on June 11–12, 2013, as well as from detailed responses from the public to targeted questions that were published on www.nano.gov from June 7, 2013 to June 14, 2013.[4] The draft strategic plan was posted on www.nano.gov for a 30-day public comment period from November 19 to December 18, 2013.

Thus informed by feedback and recommendations from a broad array of stakeholders, this strategic plan represents the consensus of the participating agencies as to the high-level goals and priorities of the NNI and specific objectives for at least the next three years. It serves as an integrated, interagency approach that informs the nanotechnology-specific strategic plans of NNI agencies (e.g., the *Strategic Plan for NIOSH Nanotechnology Research and Guidance*,[5] the EPA's *Nanomaterial Research Strategy*,[6] and the FDA's *Nanotechnology Regulatory Science Research Plan*[7]). Accordingly, the strategic plan provides the framework within which each agency will carry out its own mission-related nanotechnology programs and that will sustain coordination of interagency activities. It describes the four overarching goals of the NNI, the major program component areas (PCAs)—established in 2004 and revised in 2013—that are used to broadly track the categories of investments needed to ensure the success of the Initiative, and the near-term objectives that provide concrete steps toward collectively achieving the NNI vision and goals. Finally, the plan describes collaborative interagency activities. These include Nanotechnology Signature Initiatives (NSIs), which serve as a model of specifically targeted and closely coordinated interagency, cross-sector collaboration designed to accelerate innovation in areas of national priority. The first three NSIs, launched in 2010, are focused on solar energy, sustainable manufacturing, and next-generation electronics. Two additional NSIs on informatics and sensors were introduced in 2012.

---

[3] See Appendix A for details on external reviews and assessments of the NNI.
[4] More information about the workshop and stakeholder input is available in Appendix B.
[5] www.cdc.gov/niosh/docs/2010-105
[6] www.epa.gov/nanoscience/files/nanotech_research_strategy_final.pdf
[7] www.fda.gov/ScienceResearch/SpecialTopics/Nanotechnology/ucm273325.htm

The 21st Century Nanotechnology Research and Development Act of 2003[8] calls for the NNI Strategic Plan to be updated triennially. The first NNI Strategic Plan in 2004 outlined the Initiative's management, vision and goals, and PCAs, as well as technical areas addressed. The 2007 plan further developed the concepts presented in 2004 with an emphasis both on the coordination of the Initiative and on critical research needs. The 2011 plan introduced objectives under the four goals as well as the NSI program. The plan presented here updates and replaces the 2011 plan. Revised PCAs are included, as is an enhanced emphasis on key research priorities through the NSIs.

Vision and Goals

The vision of the NNI is a future in which the ability to understand and control matter at the nanoscale leads to a revolution in technology and industry that benefits society. The NNI expedites the discovery, development, and deployment of nanoscale science, engineering, and technology to serve the public good through a program of coordinated research and development aligned with the missions of the participating agencies. In order to realize the NNI vision, the NNI agencies are working collectively toward the following four goals:

Goal 1: Advance a world-class nanotechnology research and development program.

The NNI enables U.S. leadership in nanotechnology R&D by stimulating discovery and innovation. The Initiative expands the boundaries of knowledge and develops technologies through a comprehensive program of R&D. The NNI agencies invest at the frontiers and intersections of many disciplines, including biology, chemistry, engineering, materials science, and physics. The interest in nanotechnology arises from its potential to significantly impact numerous fields, including aerospace, agriculture, energy, the environment, healthcare, information technology, homeland security, national defense, and transportation systems.

Goal 2: Foster the transfer of new technologies into products for commercial and public benefit.

Nanotechnology contributes to U.S. competitiveness and national security by improving existing products and processes and by creating new ones. The NNI agencies implement strategies that maximize the economic and public benefits of their investments in nanotechnology, based on understanding the fundamental science and responsibly translating this knowledge into practical applications.

Goal 3: Develop and sustain educational resources, a skilled workforce, and a dynamic infrastructure and toolset to advance nanotechnology.

A skilled science and engineering workforce, leading-edge instrumentation, and state-of-the-art facilities are essential to advancing nanotechnology R&D. Educational programs and resources are required to inform the general public, decision makers, and other stakeholders (including regulators, managers, insurers, and financiers), and to produce the next generation of nanotechnologists—that is, the researchers, inventors, engineers, and technicians who drive discovery, innovation, industry, and manufacturing.

---

[8] Pub. L. No. 108-153, § 7501, 117 Stat. 1923 (2003).

Goal 4: Support responsible development of nanotechnology.
The NNI aims to responsibly develop nanotechnology by maximizing the benefits of nanotechnology while, at the same time, developing an understanding of potential risks and the means to assess and manage them. Specifically, the NNI agencies pursue a program of research, education, collaboration, and communication focused on the environmental, health, and safety (EHS) implications of nanotechnology—informed by the interagency *2011 NNI EHS Research Strategy*[9]—and on broader societal dimensions of nanotechnology development. In addition, NNI agency efforts are guided by two memoranda from the Emerging Technologies Interagency Policy Coordination Committee (ETIPC)[10] that outline broad principles for regulation and oversight of emerging technologies and, more specifically, nanotechnology.[11,12] Responsible development requires engagement with universities, industry, government agencies (local, regional, state, and Federal), nongovernmental organizations, and other communities.

As the NNI agencies work toward realizing the NNI vision, success will not be defined as a static endpoint. Rather, success will be measured by continual and substantive progress toward the four goals. For example, progress may be reflected in each of the goals by the following: Goal 1—the frontiers of knowledge are substantially advanced through a robust and interdisciplinary R&D program; Goal 2—innovative nanotechnology-enabled products (NEPs) are commercialized by a vibrant and competitive industry sector; Goal 3—the general public has access to information on fundamental nanotechnology concepts, a skilled nanotechnology workforce is trained, and scientists/engineers are aware of and have access to state-of-the-art facilities; and Goal 4—tools for characterizing hazard and exposure are developed, agencies enhance their capacity to evaluate the application of nanotechnology, and relevant EHS information is disseminated among stakeholders.

Agency Interests in the NNI

The NSET Subcommittee was established in July 2000 as part of the NSTC CoT to facilitate interagency collaboration on nanoscale R&D and to provide a framework for setting Federal R&D budget priorities related to nanotechnology. Moreover, the NSET Subcommittee provides a platform for communication, collaboration, and coordination that continues to promote the engagement of all participating agencies, including those with an interest but no targeted funding in nanotechnology. In the following sections, the agencies describe their individual interests in nanotechnology R&D and the NNI, as they collectively contribute to the welfare of the Nation and to their respective agency missions and responsibilities.[13]

Consumer Product Safety Commission (CPSC)

CPSC, in cooperation with Federal partners, analyzes the use and safety of nanotechnology in consumer products. In order to meet identified data needs, the CPSC staff has met with and

---

[9] www.nano.gov/node/681

[10] The ETIPC is described more thoroughly in the "Coordination and Assessment" chapter.

[11] www.whitehouse.gov/sites/default/files/microsites/ostp/etipc-memo-3-11-2011.pdf

[12] www.whitehouse.gov/sites/default/files/omb/inforeg/for-agencies/nanotechnology-regulation-and-oversight-principles.pdf

[13] The latest information on the nanotechnology activities of NNI agencies is available at www.nano.gov.

collaborates with staff at a number of Federal agencies in areas of mutual interest where collaboration would be beneficial and support the respective missions of each agency. More consumer products are using compounds or materials that have been produced using nanotechnologies that directly manipulate matter at the atomic level and produce materials that could not have been produced in the past.

Nanomaterials with the same chemical composition as larger-scale materials may demonstrate different physical and chemical properties and may behave differently in the environment and the human body. CPSC has developed an internal nanotechnology team composed of various technical experts (e.g., engineers, toxicologists, and economists) to advise the Commission on the safe use of nanotechnology in consumer products. As part of the NNI, the CPSC nanotechnology team participates in the interagency collection and analysis of data and in the development of reports that focus on the potential EHS issues associated with the use of nanotechnology.

Department of Commerce (DOC)

DOC participates in the NNI to promote job creation, economic growth, sustainable development, and improved standards of living for all Americans by working in partnership with businesses, universities, communities, and our Nation's workers. The Department touches the daily lives of the American people in many ways, with a wide range of responsibilities where nanotechnology is important, including trade, economic development, technology, entrepreneurship and business development, environmental stewardship, and statistical research and analysis. The Bureau of Industry and Security (BIS), Economic Development Administration (EDA), National Institute of Standards and Technology (NIST), and U.S. Patent and Trademark Office (USPTO) are active participants in the NSET Subcommittee. Their engagement informs the department-wide coordination of nanotechnology trade and economic policy, R&D, standards activities, and the protection of intellectual property across the Federal Government.

Bureau of Industry and Security (BIS)

The interagency coordination provided by the NNI enables BIS to stay apprised of new nanotechnology advancements that may present national security challenges and that may provide opportunities for companies in the national defense industrial base. Further, the NNI creates mechanisms (e.g., through regular meetings of the NSET Subcommittee) for BIS to share information about national security needs and challenges with other Federal agencies. BIS may also exercise its statutory data collection authority, as needed, in support of the NNI vision. Together, these exchanges support the BIS mission to advance U.S. national security, foreign policy, and economic objectives by ensuring an effective export control and treaty compliance system and promoting continued U.S. strategic technology leadership.

Economic Development Administration (EDA)

The mission of EDA is to lead the Federal economic development agenda by promoting innovation and competitiveness, preparing American regions for growth and success in the worldwide economy. Economic development results in a sustained increase in prosperity and quality of life through innovation, lowered transaction costs, and the utilization of capabilities toward the responsible production and diffusion of goods and services. The vision and four goals of the NNI Strategic Plan align strongly with EDA's mission and leading-edge economic development policy. The NSET Subcommittee provides a venue for EDA to understand the current state of nanotechnology development and to collaborate across the Federal Government to increase the rate and efficiency of nanotechnology commercialization efforts that originate in and near our Nation's research laboratories. EDA's support for commercialization includes funding for innovation centers, coordination with universities and Federal labs, collaborative funding opportunities with other Federal agencies, and technical assistance and capacity building for regional innovation ecosystems that support entrepreneurs. Further, EDA funding priorities include support for innovation in nanotechnology-relevant sectors such as advanced and additive manufacturing, energy, green growth, and others.

National Institute of Standards and Technology (NIST)

Advancing nanoscale measurement science, standards, and technology is an important component of NIST's mission to promote U.S. innovation and industrial competitiveness. From leading cutting-edge research, to providing world-class user facilities, to coordinating the development of standards that promote trade and enable regulation of NEPs, NIST's nanotechnology program directly impacts priorities important to the Nation's economy and well-being. The NNI-related research conducted in NIST's laboratories and user facilities develops measurements, standards, and data crucial to a wide range of industries and Federal agencies, from the development of new measurement and fabrication methods necessary for advanced manufacturing to the development of the reference materials and data necessary to accurately measure key nanomaterial properties needed for the responsible development and use of nanotechnology. NIST further supports the U.S. nanotechnology enterprise through its two user facilities, the NIST Center for Neutron Research (NCNR) and the Center for Nanoscale Science and Technology (CNST). The NCNR provides access to a broad range of world-class neutron scattering tools for characterizing the atomic- and nanometer-scale structure and dynamics of materials. As the Department of Commerce's nanotechnology user facility, the CNST enables innovation by providing rapid access to the tools needed to make and measure nanostructures, with a particular emphasis on helping industry.

The NNI has enabled NIST to prioritize and coordinate nanotechnology research in numerous areas, most notably in nanoelectronics, nanomanufacturing, and energy, as well as the environmental, health, and safety aspects of nanomaterials (nanoEHS). NIST is working closely with other NNI agencies in planning and implementing the NSIs. Through activities of the NSET Subcommittee's Nanotechnology Environmental and Health Implications (NEHI) Working Group, NIST receives input from a broad range of stakeholders on the critical measurement science and measurement tools—protocols, standards, instruments, models, and validated data—required for risk assessment and management of ENMs and NEPs. This input is essential to the development and implementation of NIST's nanoEHS program, including its goals and milestones.

NIST staff members participate widely in nanotechnology-related standards development and international cooperation activities in order to promote transfer of NIST research, technology, and measurement services and to advance NNI objectives within the Department of Commerce mission. NIST staff also participates and provides leadership roles in many key collaborative activities such as the Organisation for Economic Co-operation and Development's (OECD) Working Party on Manufactured Nanomaterials, and in the development of nanotechnology standards in international forums, such as the International Organization for Standardization (ISO) Technical Committee 229, the International Electrotechnical Commission (IEC) Technical Committee 113, and ASTM International Committee E56. Interagency coordination and information-sharing related to these activities is facilitated through the NSET Subcommittee and the NNI's Coordinator for Global Issues.

U.S. Patent and Trademark Office (USPTO)

The strength and vitality of the U.S. economy depends directly on effective mechanisms that protect new ideas and investments in innovation and creativity. USPTO is at the cutting edge of the Nation's technological progress and achievement as the Federal agency responsible for granting patents, registering trademarks, and providing intellectual property policy advice and guidance to the Executive Branch. Through its participation in the NNI and work with other agencies in the NSET Subcommittee, USPTO has made several improvements to its processes to keep pace with the rapid advances being made in this area. Notably, USPTO adopted the NNI definition of nanotechnology in its development of the first detailed, patent-related nanotechnology classification hierarchy of any major intellectual property office in the world. USPTO also has used the networking and information-sharing opportunities presented by participation in the NNI to establish nanotechnology-related training opportunities for patent examiners. USPTO has significantly contributed to the NNI by providing advice on patent and other intellectual-property-related matters as well as contributing a variety of nanotechnology-related patent data, which have been used as benchmarks to analyze nanotechnology development and to perform trend analysis of nanotechnology patenting activity in the United States and globally.

Department of Defense (DOD)

DOD leadership considers nanotechnology to have high and growing potential to contribute to the warfighting capabilities of the Nation. Because of the broad and interdisciplinary nature of nanotechnology, DOD leadership views it as an enabling technology area that should receive the highest level of Department attention and coordination. The vision of the Assistant Secretary of Defense for Research and Engineering includes nano science and engineering as one of six high interest basic science areas, along with synthetic biology, quantum information science, cognitive neuroscience, human behavior modeling, and novel engineered materials. The definition, potential, and challenges of nanotechnology are described by DOD in the following terms: the science of materials on the atomic scale makes possible new classes of electronics and sensors, chemical catalysts, high-strength materials, and energetic materials. Challenges include developing new ENMs, functionalizing them when necessary, and incorporating them into devices. More specifically, nanotechnology is an enabling technology for new classes of sensors (such as novel focal plane arrays and chemical/biological threat sensors), communications, and information processing systems needed for qualitative improvements in persistent surveillance. DOD also invests in nanotechnology for advanced energetic materials, photocatalytic coatings, active microelectronic devices, structural fibers, strength- and toughness-enhancing additives, advanced processing, and a wide array of other promising applications. The DOD nanotechnology efforts are based on coordinated planning and federated execution among the military departments and agencies (e.g., the Defense Advanced Research Projects Agency and the Defense Threat Reduction Agency). Although DOD does not establish funding targets for nanotechnology specifically, its support for nanotechnology-related R&D has remained robust through the competitive success of nanotechnology-related efforts in core research planning, technology development solicitations, and other programs, such as Small Business Innovation Research (SBIR) and the Multidisciplinary University Research Initiative.

DOD was among the initial participating agencies in the NNI and the NSET Subcommittee and considers the Initiative and its formal coordination forums to have been valuable as a means to facilitate technology planning, coordination, and communication among the Federal agencies. The meetings and workshops hosted or facilitated by the NSET Subcommittee and NNI participants help to identify and define options and opportunities that materially contribute to DOD planning activities and program formulation. The transparency that is enabled by the NNI is viewed as symmetrically beneficial to DOD, the other agencies, and the many private-sector stakeholders in the broad arena of nanoscience, nanotechnology, and nanotechnology-enabled applications.

Department of Education (DOEd)

DOEd faces major challenges in a number of education-related areas, including a need for more graduates and researchers in areas of science, technology, engineering, and mathematics (STEM) education. By providing working groups, regular NSET Subcommittee meetings, and interagency communication channels, the NNI provides a mechanism for DOEd to better collaborate with other relevant agencies, such as the National Science Foundation, which makes substantial investments in nanotechnology-related education, and the Department of Labor, which follows trends in workforce needs.

Department of Energy (DOE)

DOE leadership views nanoscience and nanotechnology as having a vitally important role to play in solving the energy and climate-change challenges faced by the Nation. This broad and diverse field of R&D will likely have a dramatic impact on future technologies for solar energy collection and conversion, energy storage, alternative fuels, and energy efficiency, to name just a few. DOE has participated in the NNI since its inception and maintains a strong commitment to the Initiative, which has served as an effective and valuable way of spotlighting needs and targeting resources in this critical emerging area of science and technology. The NNI continues to provide a focus for overall investment in physical sciences, a crucial locus for interagency communication and collaboration, and an impetus for coordinated planning. The research and infrastructure successes spurred by the NNI have made the United States a world leader in this area, with significant national benefit.

DOE funding includes investments in fundamental phenomena and processes, ENMs, nanotechnology-enabled devices, and major research facilities. In the latter category, the DOE investment is significantly larger than that of any other agency, due primarily to the operation of five Nanoscale Science Research Centers (NSRCs) located at DOE laboratories. The NSRCs operate as user facilities, with access based on submission of proposals that are reviewed by independent evaluation boards and provided at no cost for nonproprietary work. The NSRCs support synthesis, processing, fabrication, and analysis at the nanoscale and are designed to be state-of-the-art user centers for interdisciplinary nanoscale research, serving as an integral part of DOE's comprehensive nanoscience program that encompasses new science, new tools, and new computing capabilities.

Department of Health and Human Services (DHHS)

DHHS participates in the National Nanotechnology Initiative as part of its mission to protect the health of all Americans and provide essential human services. The Food and Drug Administration (FDA), National Institute for Occupational Safety and Health (NIOSH), and National Institutes of Health (NIH) contribute to the NSET Subcommittee to address a range of priorities relevant to the NNI. DHHS also contributes to the NNI EHS efforts toward responsible development of nanotechnology through a variety of mechanisms, most notably the NEHI Working Group of the NSET Subcommittee.

Food and Drug Administration (FDA)

The use of nanotechnology can alter the safety, effectiveness, performance, and/or quality of FDA-regulated products. For this reason, FDA is interested in additional scientific information and tools to help better detect and predict potential effects of such changes on human or animal health.

FDA investments will continue to enable the agency to address questions related to the safety, effectiveness, quality, and/or regulatory status of products that contain ENMs or otherwise involve the use of nanotechnology; develop models for safety and efficacy assessment; and study the behavior of nanomaterials in biological systems and their effects on human or animal health. These investments support FDA's mission to protect and promote public health and help support the responsible development of nanotechnology.

FDA has developed a regulatory science program in nanotechnology to foster the responsible development of FDA-regulated products that may contain ENMs or otherwise involve the application of nanotechnology. The FDA program establishes tools, methods, and data to assist in regulatory decision-making while providing in-house scientific expertise and capacity that is responsive to nanotechnology-related FDA-regulated products.

The Office of the Commissioner, in partnership with the FDA Nanotechnology Task Force, facilitates communication and cooperation across the agency on nanotechnology regulatory science research, both within FDA and with national and international stakeholders. The FDA Nanotechnology Task Force provides the overall coordination of FDA's nanotechnology regulatory science research efforts in the following programmatic investment areas: (1) scientific staff development and professional training; (2) laboratory and product-testing capacity; and (3) collaborative and interdisciplinary regulatory science research.

As needed and appropriate, FDA continues to foster and develop collaborative relationships with other Federal agencies through participation in the NNI and the NSET Subcommittee, as well as with regulatory agencies, international organizations, healthcare professionals, industry, consumers, and other stakeholders. These collaborations allow information to be exchanged efficiently and serve to identify research needs related to the use of ENMs in FDA-regulated products.

Although FDA activities are relevant to all four NNI goals, FDA efforts are primarily focused on Goal 4, to support responsible development of nanotechnology.

National Institute for Occupational Safety and Health (NIOSH)

The National Institute for Occupational Safety and Health is responsible for conducting research and providing guidance to protect the health and safety of people at work. Workers are generally the first people in society to be exposed to the hazards of an emerging technology, and nanotechnology is no exception. The workplaces where ENMs and NEPs are developed, investigated, manufactured, used, and disposed of are quite varied and span all economic sectors. NIOSH conducts focused research on hazard identification, exposure assessment, risk characterization, and risk management to protect the health and safety of workers, develop effective recommendations, and promote responsible development of the technology. In order to meet the need for a unified approach to this complex research challenge, the NIOSH Nanotechnology Research Center (NTRC) was chartered. NTRC provides internal coordination of research and serves as an interface point for NNI participating agencies.

NIOSH toxicology studies continue to provide better understanding of the ways in which some types of ENMs may enter the body and interact with the body's organ systems. The scope of these research efforts has expanded beyond the few nanoparticle types evaluated at the start of the NIOSH nanotechnology research program. A key component of this effort is to understand the characteristics and properties relevant for predicting potential health risks. The toxicology studies have served as a starting point to identify the priority materials for further risk assessment, exposure evaluations, and development of risk management practices.

NIOSH field investigators continue to assess exposure to ENMs, including a focused effort on carbon nanotubes, in a growing number of workplaces. However, more data are needed on the full extent and magnitude of workers' exposures to broad categories of ENMs in workplaces that manufacture or use ENMs, nanostructures, and nanodevices. NIOSH field investigators plan to expand the scope of assessment and the number and type of facilities that can be assessed.

Controlling worker exposure to ENMs is one of the first steps in a risk-based approach to responsible development of nanotechnology. NIOSH will increase its effort with private sector partners to evaluate the extent of adherence with risk management guidance, with initial focus on evaluating the effectiveness of engineering control measures. Significantly more field research is needed to address questions raised about possible human health risks in exposed nanotechnology workers and to develop guidance for medical screening and prospective epidemiologic studies.

NIOSH will continue to work with NNI agencies and a broad range of national and international private and public partners to develop research-based information and guidance to protect workers involved with ENMs. The results being produced by NIOSH will continue to serve as the foundation for meeting the critical NNI research needs related to human hazard and exposure assessment, exposure mitigation, risk assessment techniques, risk management practices, and human medical surveillance and epidemiology. NIOSH has developed formal collaborations with the National Toxicology Program (National Institute of Environmental Health Sciences, NIEHS), CPSC, DOD, and the Occupational Safety and Health Administration. It has also developed productive informal interactions with additional agencies, including the U.S. Environmental Protection Agency (EPA), NIST, DOE, and the Food and Drug Administration.

National Institutes of Health (NIH)

The National Institutes of Health is the primary Federal agency for conducting and supporting medical research. The NIH mission is to seek fundamental knowledge about the nature and behavior of living systems and the application of that knowledge to enhance health, lengthen life, and reduce the burdens of illness and disability. Toward these ends, NIH leadership realizes that advances in nanoscience and nanotechnology have the potential to make valuable contributions to biology, medicine, and related disciplines, which in turn could contribute to a new era in healthcare. The Federal agencies' R&D investments, for example, have resulted in advanced materials, tools, and nanotechnology-enabled instrumentation that can be used to study and understand biological processes in health and disease. NIH-supported R&D efforts, in particular, are bringing about new paradigms in the detection, diagnosis, and treatment of common and rare diseases, resulting in new classes of nanotherapeutics and diagnostic biomarkers, tests, and devices.

NIH became a participant in the NNI in 2001. The NNI serves as a framework within which NIH can work collaboratively with other agencies to address some of the most perplexing challenges in the development and application of nanotechnologies for biomedical applications. Through this interagency planning, coordination, and communication, scientists are addressing key challenges by:

- Understanding the manner in which nanoscale building blocks and processes integrate and assemble into larger systems and how these processes can be precisely controlled to achieve predictable outcomes.
- Learning how to design ENMs that can seamlessly and functionally integrate with tissues of the body to perform biological functions.
- Developing "top-down" and "bottom-up" engineering approaches to control properties that allow the identification, characterization, and quantification of biological molecules, chemicals, and structures involved in early-stage changes or progression in a disease state.
- Engineering complex, theranostic-based nanoparticles and nanodevices to target therapies and diagnose the progress of treatments.
- Adopting new materials, nanotechnology-enabled tools, and analytical instruments from diverse fields to support medical research.

NIH continues to support the NNI by stimulating R&D in nanoscience and nanotechnology through both intramural and extramural funding activities in all five PCAs, with major financial investments in foundational research (PCA 2) and nanotechnology-enabled applications, devices, and systems (PCA 3). For more information on specific topics funded by NIH, please visit the NIH Research Portfolio Online Reporting Tool at www.report.nih.gov. NIH plays a substantive role in developing scientific understanding of how to design ENMs for safe use in manufacturing and in medical treatments. The National Cancer Institute (NCI), for example, established the Nanotechnology Characterization Laboratory, which has developed a comprehensive assay portfolio for the assessment of the safety of nanoparticles in *in vivo* applications, and NIEHS and the National Toxicology Program have focused on assessing properties relevant to the chronic exposure of workers to ENMs. NIH institutes also support large center grants, program grants, and small businesses whose technologies or products are licensed or currently undergoing Phase I–III clinical trials.

Department of Homeland Security (DHS)

DHS interests in nanoscience are primarily focused on the application of nanoscale materials and devices that provide enhancements in component technology performance for homeland security applications. The applications for the efforts described below are in threat detection for enhanced security for aviation, mass transit, and first responders:

- *Materials toolbox:* These efforts are focused on the development of materials systems that allow systematic control of chemical and structural features from molecular scales (functional groups) through nano- and microscales. The ability to precisely tune material properties is critical for successful development of improved active sensor surfaces and analyte collection substrates as well as for development of novel sensing structures and arrays.
- *Advanced preconcentrators:* The DHS Science and Technology Directorate is currently investigating the development of high-performance preconcentrators for use in next-generation detection systems. The focus of these efforts is the development of nano- and microscale materials that enable radio-frequency and optical control of device temperature. To date, several functional prototypes have been demonstrated. Commercialization of these devices is currently being pursued.
- *Advanced sensing platforms:* Work on the development of multimodal carbon nanotube sensing platforms continues with industry partners. The emphasis of these efforts is on development of manufacturing techniques for low-cost sensor platforms.

Department of the Interior (DOI) / U.S. Geological Survey (USGS)

At USGS, nanotechnology research involves evaluating the effects of nanoparticles at various levels of biological organization, from the molecular to the ecosystem level.[14] Much of USGS nanotechnology research focuses on assessing the occurrence, fate, and effects of naturally occurring and engineered chemical contaminants in aquatic environments or on methods for detecting metal nanomaterials. Several programs provide information on nanoparticles or other contaminants, including the Contaminant Biology Program, the Toxic Substances Hydrology Program,[15] the National Research Program,[16] and the Water Resources Research Institutes.[17] The NNI, through regular NSET Subcommittee meetings and activities within the NSET working groups, provides mechanisms for USGS to share information on nanotechnology research and to collaborate with other agencies.

Department of Justice (DOJ) / National Institute of Justice (NIJ)

The NIJ investment in nanotechnology furthers DOJ's mission through the sponsorship of research that provides objective, independent, evidence-based knowledge and tools to meet the challenges of crime and justice, particularly at the state and local levels. New projects are awarded on a competitive basis; therefore, total investment may change each fiscal year. However, NIJ continues to view nanotechnology as an integral component of its R&D portfolio as applicable to criminal justice needs.

---

[14] Details at www.microbiology.usgs.gov/nanotechnology.html.
[15] toxics.usgs.gov
[16] water.usgs.gov/nrp
[17] water.usgs.gov/wrri

Department of Labor (DOL) / Occupational Safety and Health Administration (OSHA)

OSHA plays an integral role in nanotechnology by protecting the Nation's workforce. OSHA accomplishes its mission by collaborating and sharing information with other Federal agencies through NNI activities and NSET Subcommittee meetings. As part of this effort, OSHA's goal is to educate employers on their responsibility to protect workers and to educate workers on safe practices in handling ENMs. OSHA is developing guidance and educational materials promoting worker safety and health that will be shared with the public directly and through the NNI.

In addition, OSHA is interested in ensuring responsible and sustainable nanotechnology by promoting and developing manufacturing processes that take safety and health into consideration from the design of manufacturing systems throughout the entire life cycle of the material in use, wherever there is potential for worker exposure. To achieve this objective, OSHA is participating in the nanomanufacturing NSI and collaborating with EPA and NIOSH to promote sustainable development in the manufacturing process. This involves development of nanomanufacturing processes that take into account exposure control measures to eliminate or reduce worker exposure from the outset.

OSHA is also involved in the Nanotechnology Knowledge Infrastructure NSI, participating in collaboration with other agencies in creating a robust data and information infrastructure. Sharing information on nanotechnology health-related data supports OSHA's goal to develop materials promoting worker safety and health.

Department of State (DOS)

DOS actively participates in the NNI in order to identify and promote multilateral and bilateral scientific activities that support U.S. foreign policy objectives, protect national security interests, advance economic interests, and foster environmental protection. International scientific collaboration enhances existing U.S. research, development, and innovation programs. Nanotechnology's enormous potential to address global challenges relating to the environment, energy, and health renders it an ideal subject for collaboration on precompetitive and noncompetitive research. DOS assists NNI agencies in establishing partnerships with counterpart institutions abroad by holding regular joint committee meetings with representatives from over fifty countries. These meetings are governed by binding science and technology agreements that facilitate exchange of scientific results, provide for protection and allocation of intellectual property rights and benefit sharing, facilitate access for researchers, address taxation issues, and respond to the complex set of issues associated with economic development, domestic security, and regional stability. DOS also leads efforts in the Working Party on Nanotechnology (WPN) of the OECD, the Strategic Approach to International Chemicals Management (SAICM), and other international organizations that support the responsible development of nanotechnology.

Department of Transportation (DOT) / Federal Highway Administration (FHWA)

FHWA sees great promise in the application of nanotechnology to help solve long-term transportation research needs in support of DOT's strategic goals: Safety, Livable Communities, State of Good Repair, Economic Competitiveness, and Environmental Sustainability. By strategically investing in focused research areas and leveraging investments in nanoscale technology by other NNI partners and Federal agencies, industry, and academia, FHWA aims to accelerate the capability to provide safer, more efficient, longer-lasting highway transportation systems. FHWA's Exploratory Advanced Research

Program is investing in nanoscale research to address key highway research issues in infrastructure, safety, operations, and the environment. Nanotechnology promises breakthroughs in multiple areas, offering a potential for synergy and benefits across many traditional highway research focus areas.

The development of innovative materials and coatings can deliver significant improvements in durability, performance, and resiliency of highway and transportation infrastructure components. Nanoscale engineering of traditional transportation infrastructure materials (e.g., steel, concrete, asphalt, and other cementitious materials, as well as recycled forms of these materials) offers great promise. Developments in nanoscale sensors and devices may provide cost-effective opportunities to embed and employ structural health monitoring systems to continuously monitor corrosion, material degradation, and performance of structures and pavements under service loads and conditions. In addition, these developments might provide multifunctional properties to traditional infrastructure materials, such as the ability to generate or transmit energy. Nanoscale sensors and devices may also enable a cost-effective infrastructure that communicates with vehicle-based systems to assist drivers with tasks such as maintaining lane position, avoiding collisions at intersections, and modifying or coordinating travel behavior to mitigate congestion or adverse environmental impacts. Other environmental applications include sensors to monitor mobile source pollutants and air, water, and soil quality.

FHWA's long-term strategy is to continue targeted investment in select areas while building an appreciation for highway research needs with NNI agencies and the broader nanoscale research community in order to augment longstanding partnerships and make significant progress toward improving the Nation's highway and transportation systems.

Department of the Treasury (DOTreas)

DOTreas works through the NSET Subcommittee to help the NNI achieve its vision congruent with that of DOTreas: to serve the American people and strengthen national security by managing the Federal Government's finances effectively; to promote economic growth and stability; and to ensure the safety, soundness, and security of U.S. and international financial systems. DOTreas monitors those aspects of developing nanotechnology that could most effectively assist the execution of its role as the steward of the U.S. economic and financial systems and as an influential participant in the global economy. DOTreas seeks to assess and utilize nanotechnology in the discharge of its responsibilities, including advising the President on economic and financial issues, encouraging sustainable economic growth, and fostering improved governance in financial institutions. It seeks to harness those aspects of nanotechnology R&D that will allow it to better operate and maintain systems that are critical to the Nation's financial infrastructure, such as the production of coin and currency. Interactions with the NSET Subcommittee help DOTreas as it endeavors to capture developments in nanoscale science and engineering that are changing the parameters of its domestic and international operations, particularly those impacting its critical national security-related activities in implementing economic sanctions against foreign threats to the United States, identifying and targeting the financial support networks of national security threats, improving the safeguards of U.S. financial systems, and creating new economic and job opportunities to promote economic growth and stability at home and abroad.

Environmental Protection Agency (EPA)

EPA's interest in the NNI is to collaborate to better understand the implications and applications of ENMs to help protect human health and the environment. EPA's main interest is to understand how ENMs can be designed and used to minimize potential adverse public health or environmental impacts. Second, EPA is interested in the potential of using advances in nanotechnology to improve the environment, including its use for environmental sensing, remediating pollutants, and for developing more environmentally friendly substances. Both interests focus on the sustainable use of nanotechnology.

Nanotechnology offers potentially transformative capabilities for a vast array of products and processes, including those that enhance environmental quality and sustainability. To help nanotechnology create maximum societal benefits and to minimize its potential environmental impacts, EPA collaborates with Federal partners within the NSET Subcommittee, and with international organizations such as OECD, to bridge research gaps, address critical issues such as regulatory needs and test guidelines, and communicate information about nanotechnology to all interested stakeholders.

Intelligence Community (IC) / Office of the Director of National Intelligence (ODNI)

There are several agencies within IC that conduct nanotechnology R&D. The National Reconnaissance Office (NRO) has an R&D program that focuses on nanoelectronics, nanomaterials, and energy generation and storage using nanotechnologies.

In nanoelectronics, both analog and digital, the emphasis is on ultralow power for terrestrial data centers and radiation-hardened ultralow power for satellites. Carbon-based nanoelectronics are compatible with today's microelectronics and the foundries that produce them. A major focus going forward will be on ultradense, ultralow-power nonvolatile memory for saving power in data centers and satellites, replacement for today's silicon logic, and advanced linear analog nanoelectronics for next-generation communications and radar systems. These nanoelectronics will transform today's systems into advanced capabilities that will solve tomorrow's IC challenges.

ENMs, including carbon-based sheets and threads, will be used to develop advanced ultralight, ultrastrong composites for satellites, unmanned aircraft, and advanced body armor. Carbon-based threads will be used to develop novel ultralightweight cables and wires for satellites, aircraft, and data centers that reduce weight by as much as 80% and deliver more data signals and power than conventional copper wires and cables.

Nanotechnologies are being applied to solar cells to achieve 35% efficiency in the near term and develop 40% to 47% efficiencies in the medium term for use in space. With the application of 10 to 1000 times normal sunlight (concentration), 52% to 61% efficiency can be achieved for terrestrial use, as defined by current research. Carbon-based nanomaterials are also being developed for advanced lithium-ion batteries with 3 to 5 times more power, more rapid rechargeability, and much lighter weight than current lithium ion batteries.

Nanotechnology provides the IC with transformative and game-changing capabilities not achievable with conventional electronics, materials, or power technologies, and with greatly reduced size, weight, power, and cost. The NSET Subcommittee provides an open forum where agencies can describe their nanotechnology portfolios to other agencies, making them aware of progress achieved. It also affords the opportunity to collaborate to further accelerate nanotechnology R&D, prototyping, nanomanufacturing, *in situ* and post-product metrology, and final transition to acquisition programs.

National Aeronautics and Space Administration (NASA)

The three prime drivers for NASA's aerospace R&D activities are to (1) reduce vehicle weight, (2) enhance performance, and (3) improve safety, durability, and reliability. Nanotechnology is a tool to address each of these drivers. Nanotechnology research at NASA is focused in four areas: engineered materials and structures; energy generation, storage, and distribution; electronics, sensors, and devices; and propulsion. This research is conducted through a combination of in-house activities at NASA research and flight centers, competitively funded research with universities and industry, and collaborations with other agencies, universities, and industry. Through the University Research Centers Program, NASA has also funded nanotechnology research at minority-serving institutions, including the Center for Advanced Nanoscale Materials at the University of Puerto Rico and the High Performance Polymers and Composites Center at Clark Atlanta University. A major emphasis of NASA's nanotechnology R&D is on transitioning nanotechnology discoveries into mission applications.

NASA has participated in the NNI since its inception and is committed to partnering with other participating agencies to identify key technical challenges in nanotechnology R&D, focus resources to address these challenges, and accelerate the development of nanotechnology breakthroughs and their translation into commercial products.

National Science Foundation (NSF)

NSF supports fundamental nanoscale science and engineering in and across all disciplines. It supports formal and informal nanotechnology education and physical research infrastructure in academic institutions. It also advances nanotechnology innovation through a variety of translational research programs and by partnering with industry, states, and other agencies.

The NSF nanotechnology investment in 2013 supported over 5,000 active projects, over 30 research centers, and several infrastructure networks for device development, computation, and education. It impacted over 10,000 students and teachers. Approximately 150 small businesses have been funded to perform research and product development in nanotechnology through the SBIR and Small Business Technology Transfer (STTR) programs. NSF's nanotechnology research is supported primarily through grants to individuals, teams, and centers at U.S. academic institutions. The efforts in team and center projects have been particularly fruitful because nanoscale research and education are inherently interdisciplinary pursuits, often combining elements of materials science, engineering, chemistry, computer science, physics, and biology.

Fundamental changes envisioned through nanotechnology require a long-term R&D vision. NSF sponsored the first initiative dedicated to nanoparticles in 1991 and the 1997–1999 Partnership in Nanotechnology program, and it produced the 1999 interagency report *Nanotechnology Research Directions: Vision for Nanotechnology in the Next Decade*,[18] which was adopted as an official NSTC document in 2000. NSF continues to push the frontiers of science and technology innovations through

---

[18] www.nano.gov/node/948

continual interaction with the nanotechnology community, new programs, and ongoing evaluation of current investments. The NSF-led study *Nanotechnology Research Directions for Societal Needs in 2020* was released in 2010.[19] With input from academic, industry, and government experts from over 35 countries, the report addresses the progress and impact of nanotechnology since 2000 as well as the vision and research directions for nanotechnology in the next ten years. Further, convergence of nanotechnology with other technologies and areas of application have been analyzed in the NSF-led 2013 report developed in collaboration with NIH, EPA, DOD, NASA, and the U.S. Department of Agriculture (USDA), *Convergence of Knowledge, Technology, and Society.*[20]

NSF supports the NSIs through core programs and new solicitations. NSF requested additional funds in 2014 for nanomanufacturing to support new concepts for high-rate synthesis and processing of nanostructures, nanostructured catalysts, nanobiotechnology methods, and methods to fabricate devices, assemble them into systems, and then further assemble them into larger-scale structures of relevance to industry. EHS implications of nanotechnology, including development of predictive toxicity of nanomaterials and rigorous experiments to develop models for nanomaterial exposures in the environment, will be investigated in three dedicated multidisciplinary centers and in over 60 other smaller groups.

NSF also has a focus on addressing education and societal dimensions of nanotechnology. Education-related activities include development of materials for schools, curricula for nanoscience and engineering, new teaching tools, undergraduate programs, technical training, and public outreach programs. The Nanoscale Informal Science Education Network is a national network for nanotechnology education public outreach supported by NSF. Research directed at identifying and quantifying the broad implications of nanotechnology for society, including social, economic, workforce, educational, ethical, and legal implications, is investigated in small groups and in the Nanotechnology in Society Network.

Nuclear Regulatory Commission (NRC)

The mission of NRC is to license and regulate the Nation's civilian use of byproduct, source, and special nuclear materials in order to protect public health and safety, promote the common defense and security, and protect the environment. NRC's scope of responsibility includes regulation of commercial nuclear power plants; research, test, and training reactors; nuclear fuel cycle facilities; medical, academic, and industrial uses of radioactive materials; and transport, storage, and disposal of radioactive materials and waste. In addition, NRC licenses the import and export of radioactive materials and works to enhance nuclear safety and security throughout the world.

As a regulatory agency, NRC does not typically sponsor fundamental research or product development. Rather, NRC is focused in part on confirmatory research to verify the safe application of new technologies in the civilian nuclear industry. Currently the agency's focus with respect to nanotechnology is to monitor developments that might be applied within the nuclear industry to help NRC carry out its oversight role.

---

[19] www.wtec.org/nano2
[20] www.wtec.org/NBIC2

U.S. Department of Agriculture (USDA)

Nanotechnology has the potential to impact all areas that the U.S. Department of Agriculture provides leadership on: food, agriculture, natural resources, rural development, nutrition, the environment, and related issues. The Agricultural Research Service (ARS), Forest Service (FS), and National Institute of Food and Agriculture (NIFA) participate in the NSET Subcommittee to promote coordinated research, development, commercialization, education, and outreach on nanoscale science, engineering, and technology in support of a variety of applications, including cellulosic and other nano- and biomaterials, agricultural production, and human nutrition, as well as food safety and food quality. USDA also contributes to NNI EHS efforts toward responsible development and deployment of nanotechnology.

Agricultural Research Service (ARS)

ARS is USDA's chief in-house scientific research agency. ARS research leverages science and technology, including ENMs and NEPs, to enable substantial improvements in long-term agricultural production, in food safety and quality, and in human nutrition. Examples of this research include the development of nanorod-based biosensors to rapidly, accurately, and selectively identify Salmonella; the incorporation of nanoemulsions, nanoparticles, and microfibrils into edible films to develop food products with improved barrier and mechanical properties, greater nutritional value, and improved taste; and the use of nano-cantilevers to detect toxin molecules with high sensitivity.

Forest Service (FS)

Nanotechnology has enormous promise to bring about fundamental changes in and significant benefit from our Nation's use of renewable resources. For example, cellulose nanomaterials derived from trees: (1) are renewable and sustainable; (2) are produced in trees via photosynthesis from solar energy, atmospheric carbon dioxide, and water; (3) store carbon; and (4) depending upon how long cellulose-based products remain in service, are carbon negative or carbon neutral. Cellulosic nanocrystals, for example, are predicted to have strength properties comparable to Kevlar, have piezoelectric properties comparable to quartz, and can be manipulated to produce photonic structures. The USDA FS, in collaborations with Purdue University, Georgia Institute of Technology, the University of Maine, and others, has been conducting research on characterization, predictive modeling, surface modification, and development of new applications for cellulosic nanomaterials. Current global research directions in cellulose nanomaterials indicate that this material could be used for a variety of new and improved product applications, including lighter and stronger paper and paperboard products; lighter and stronger building materials; wood products with improved durability; barrier coatings; body armor; automobile and airplane composite panels; electronics; biomedical applications; and replacement of petrochemicals in plastics and composites. The U.S. forest products industry, the major supplier and a user of cellulose nanomaterials, has actively engaged with NNI agencies and programs via its industry technology alliance—the Agenda 2020—and via co-organizing workshops.

Through participation in the NNI and representation on the NSET Subcommittee, FS is partnering with other Federal entities (e.g., NIST, NSF, DOE, DOD), industry, and academia to develop the precompetitive science and technology critical to the economic and sustainable production and use of new high-value, nanotechnology-enabled forest-based products. Participation in the NNI and the NSET Subcommittee has helped create a favorable environment for increased FS investment in nanotechnology R&D. FS nanotechnology research has contributed broadly to the NNI program component areas with primary emphasis on PCA 1 (Nanotechnology Signature Initiatives/Sustainable Nanomanufacturing), PCA 3 (Nanotechnology-Enabled Applications, Devices, and Systems), and PCA 4 (Research Infrastructure and Instrumentation), with possible future investments in PCA 5 (Environment, Health, and Safety).

National Institute of Food and Agriculture (NIFA)

Established by the 2008 Farm Bill, NIFA serves the Nation's needs by supporting exemplary research, education, and extension to address challenges within its mission area. NIFA's mission is to lead food and agricultural sciences to help create a better future for the Nation and the world. NIFA's current priority areas are (1) global food security, (2) climate change, (3) sustainable bioenergy, (4) childhood obesity, and (5) food safety. Nanoscale science, engineering, and technology have demonstrated their relevance and great potential to enable revolutionary improvements in agriculture and food systems, including plant production and products; animal health, production, and products; food safety and quality; nutrition, health, and wellness; renewable bioenergy and bio-based products; natural resources and the environment; agriculture systems and technology; and agricultural economics and rural communities.

NIFA's predecessor agency (Cooperative State Research, Education, and Extension Service, or CSREES) was among the early participating agencies in the NSET Subcommittee, joining in 2002, and that agency (later, NIFA) has actively participated in and contributed to NNI activities ever since. The NNI provides a solid platform on which NIFA can effectively explore opportunities in nanoscience and nanotechnology to address critical societal challenges facing agriculture and food systems through coordination, collaboration, and leveraging resources with other Federal agencies. Scientific discoveries and technological breakthroughs inspire agricultural and food scientists to seek novel solutions. The extensive infrastructure networks developed by the NNI agencies enhance the productivity and expand the capability of agricultural and food science R&D in academia and industry. NIFA actively contributes to and benefits significantly from its participation in the NNI activities to identify research gaps and opportunities through workshops and discussions, to support public engagement and communication, to facilitate public–private partnerships in close collaboration with industry, and to participate in and promote international information exchanges and cooperation. NIFA also supports multiagency joint research efforts of common interest and importance as appropriate to its mission, goals, and objectives. The agency's nanotechnology programs have broadly contributed to the NNI, with primary emphasis on Nanotechnology Signature Initiatives (PCA 1); Foundational Research (PCA 2); Nanotechnology-Enabled Applications, Devices, and Systems (PCA 3); and Environment, Health, and Safety (PCA 5). NIFA's SBIR program also supports innovative nanotechnology R&D throughout its broad topic areas.

U.S. International Trade Commission (USITC)

The USITC representative attends NSET Subcommittee and working group meetings to keep the Commission abreast of current trends and issues related to nanotechnology that may have the potential to impact international trade. Upon request, the USITC representative may provide technical support to the NSET Subcommittee.

Goals and Objectives

The NNI vision is supported by the four NNI goals. All four are equally critical to the success of the NNI and are interdependent. This interconnection is specifically recognized in the following sections that describe shared NNI objectives, organized by NNI goal. Recurring themes that are particularly relevant for the realization of these objectives include the need for consensus standards; education and training; consideration of ethical, legal, and societal implications; public engagement; and environmental, health, and safety research.

Based on extensive input from internal and external stakeholders, the NNI agencies have specified the objectives that follow. To the extent possible, these are specific and measurable, with targeted time frames of three to five years unless otherwise indicated. Although not all member agencies are responsible for fulfilling all objectives, the Nanoscale, Science, Engineering, and Technology (NSET) Subcommittee has identified objectives that are supported by the relevant agencies and that are ambitious yet realistic. The Subcommittee has attempted to recognize available resources and functional limits while also being far-sighted in terms of focusing on objectives that will accelerate innovation and progress toward achieving the NNI goals. NNI agencies also independently continue to contribute to the achievement of all four goals through a number of their own activities, which are reported on an annual basis in the NNI Supplement to the President's Budget.[21]

The actions and associated resources required to implement the goals of this plan will need to be pursued in the context of other U.S. Government priorities. This document is not intended as an inherent justification to seek increased budgetary authority; the goals and objectives may be achieved through reprioritization and reallocation of existing resources. It is expected that agencies will consider this document in their internal prioritization and planning processes.

Goal 1: Advance a world-class nanotechnology research and development program.

NNI agencies continue to expand the boundaries of knowledge and develop technologies through comprehensive and focused R&D. The overarching aim of Goal 1 is to advance nanoscience and nanotechnology through the implementation of the objectives described below. Progress in R&D will depend upon the availability of a skilled workforce, infrastructure, and tools (Goal 3) and will lay the foundation for responsible incorporation of nanotechnology into commercial products (Goals 2 and 4).

Goal 1 Objectives

1.1. Support R&D that extends the frontiers of nanotechnology and strengthens the intersections of scientific disciplines.

> 1.1.1. Extend the frontiers of nanotechnology with a diverse R&D portfolio that includes basic scientific research, foundational research, use-inspired research, applications research, and technology development.

---

[21] Available at www.nano.gov.

1.1.2. Strengthen the intersections of scientific disciplines by creating funding opportunities specifically targeting unique and interdependent research between disciplines.

1.1.3. Sustain a strategic and complementary research portfolio incorporating intramural and extramural programs consisting of single-investigator efforts, multi-investigator and multidisciplinary research teams, and centers and networks for focused research.

Nanotechnology offers a paradigm that crosses scientific disciplines and therefore provides a unique motivation for exploring the intersections between traditional disciplines. The broad nanotechnology R&D portfolio invests at the frontiers and intersections of many areas, including biology, chemistry, computer science, ecology, engineering, geology, materials science, medicine, physics, and the social sciences. Activities targeted toward this goal span a broad continuum, from support for basic and foundational research, through use-inspired and applications research, and into technology development. The research efforts of the NNI agencies continue to be executed through a balanced mix of funding ranging from single-investigator grants to collaborative research teams and networks, research centers, and user facilities. Research efforts also include extramural research and research within Government laboratories, each of which plays a unique and vital role in the discovery and innovation process.

1.2. Identify and support nanoscale science and technology research driven by national priorities and informed by active engagement with stakeholders.

1.2.1. Engage with academia, industry, government, and the public to gather input and feedback on federally supported research.

1.2.2. Foster stakeholder engagement and collaborations with NNI agencies via means such as matching funds, partnerships, consortia, and planning exercises.

1.2.3. Disseminate and communicate nanoscale science and technology success stories and current national priorities at public workshops and conferences.

Successful advancement and commercialization of nanotechnology (Goal 2) will depend on the scientific quality of research; better understanding of the potential environmental, health, and safety implications of nanotechnology; and cognizance of its relevance and competitiveness in the marketplace. NNI agencies will continue to work with academia and across industry sectors to gather input and feedback on Federal research. Continuous engagement will facilitate the effective transition of nanotechnology from discovery to the marketplace, and direct collaborations will establish meaningful long-term relationships to advance this field. Furthermore, given the vast body of research in nanotechnology supported by NNI agencies, it is incumbent upon these agencies, assisted by the National Nanotechnology Coordination Office, to ensure that recent successes and the current national priorities are adequately communicated in national forums and scientific conferences.

1.3. Assess the performance of the U.S. nanotechnology R&D program.

1.3.1. Identify the common attributes of successful research programs and general best practices within the NNI agencies and within other domestic and international nanotechnology R&D.

1.3.2. Develop quantitative measures of performance in coordination with existing efforts to establish metrics for innovation.

1.3.3. Explore opportunities to enhance and augment current assessment strategies.

Nanotechnology is a worldwide enterprise with significant R&D efforts underway in many countries. In order to maintain U.S. leadership, it is critical to identify the common attributes that define successful nanotechnology research programs. Additionally, NNI agencies will continue to develop clearly defined metrics to measure the U.S. R&D program against those of other major economies. Efforts to quantitatively measure innovation are already underway in other areas, and the NNI and its agencies will leverage this existing work to develop appropriate metrics. Furthermore, opportunities for rapid, focused assessments of the NNI will be explored, in order to provide dynamic information exchange to enable continual refinement of nanotechnology research programs and rapid adaptation of successful approaches. For example, directors of major nanotechnology research centers (both academic and government) could be assembled to assess the most recent nanotechnology advances, in addition to the strengths and weaknesses of the investment strategies of the NNI agencies. The NNI and its

---

STAR METRICS™

STAR METRICS (www.starmetrics.nih.gov) is a Federal and research institution collaboration to create a data infrastructure and a repository of data and tools that will be useful to assess the impact of Federal R&D investments. NIH and NSF are leading the project under the auspices of OSTP, with collaboration from other agencies including EPA and the USDA. The goal of STAR METRICS is to provide a better empirical basis for science policy through the development of an enabling data infrastructure, which can be used by Federal agencies, research institutions, and researchers to document and analyze Federal investments in science. The NNI is exploring possibilities for leveraging STAR METRICS and other existing platforms, as well as potential future platforms (such as the pilot interagency effort to develop a SciENcv data platform to better link federally supported researchers with their science impacts), to assess the impacts of the U.S. nanotechnology R&D enterprise. Developing and utilizing better data and tools would enable clearer documentation of the Nation's returns on its nanotechnology investments.

---

agencies could also host focused discussions around mutually identified topics of particular interest or need to refine their nanotechnology investment strategies. Similarly, these agencies could host strategic forums to address emerging topics, such as developing reliable datasets or improving the tracking of datasets for scientific impact. These opportunities would serve as a means to establish continual dialogue with a diverse range of leading scientists and engineers working at the frontiers of nanotechnology.

1.4. Advance a portfolio of Nanotechnology Signature Initiatives (NSIs) that are each supported by three or more NNI agencies and address significant national priorities.

1.4.1. Identify potential new NSIs with input from stakeholders.

1.4.2. Conduct annual assessments of the impact and progress of each NSI to determine strategic areas of focus and the value of continuing the NSI for an additional year.

NSIs are topical areas identified by the NNI and its agencies as benefiting greatly from close and targeted interagency interactions. The NSIs spotlight key areas of national priority and provide a mechanism for enhanced collaboration to leverage R&D programs across multiple agencies. Utilizing the broad range of funding mechanisms identified in Objective 1.1, the agency activities will be coordinated within the NSIs to foster innovation and accelerate nanotechnology development. The portfolio of NSIs will be reviewed annually to determine their overall progress and the impact of the interactions catalyzed by them. These reviews will also assess each NSI relative to new opportunities to ensure that the optimum set of NSIs is supported.

Goal 2: Foster the transfer of new technologies into products for commercial and public benefit.

Since the inception of the NNI in 2001, significant advances have been made in the development of fundamental understanding of nanotechnology phenomena. While nanotechnology has found its way into a variety of commercial products (e.g., cosmetics, antimicrobial surfaces and treatments, tires, electronics, and healthcare), a continued emphasis on commercialization is needed to fully realize the benefits of nanotechnology R&D to the Nation. The purpose of Goal 2 is to establish processes and resources to facilitate the responsible transfer of nanotechnology research into practical applications and capture its benefits to national security, quality of life, economic development, and job creation.

Several factors are necessary to successfully commercialize any new technology. Scalable, repeatable, cost-effective, and high-precision manufacturing methods are required to move the technology from the laboratory into commercial products. Investments by both the public and private sectors are needed to shepherd technologies to maturity. Maximizing the benefits of nanotechnology developments to the U.S. economy requires efforts to remove barriers to global commercialization and an understanding of the potential markets for a given product.

The NNI fosters technology transfer by facilitating agency engagement with key industry sectors, providing access to the results of federally funded nanotechnology R&D and aiding in the creation of a business environment conducive to the responsible development of nanotechnology-enabled products (NEPs). Partners in this endeavor include international, regional, state, and local organizations that promote nanotechnology development as well as professional societies, trade associations, and other nongovernmental organizations.

Goal 2 Objectives

2.1. Assist the nanotechnology-based business community in understanding the Federal Government's R&D funding and regulatory environment.

> 2.1.1. Disseminate information on supporting sponsors and programs to assist transfer of nanotechnology-based technologies into Federal Government acquisition programs.

> 2.1.2. Improve public access to informational materials about resources available that support nanotechnology commercialization.

> 2.1.3. Provide informational materials, including points of contact, to explain issues pertinent to nanotechnology-enabled products and businesses.

The 2011 Presidential Memorandum on Accelerating Technology Transfer and Commercialization of Federal Research in Support of High-Growth Business[22] directs Federal agencies "to accelerate technology transfer and support private sector commercialization." NNI agencies recognize the need to raise public and business community awareness of Federal Government resources, including funding opportunities (e.g., Small Business Innovation Research and Small Business Technology Transfer Research programs), user facilities, and other resources, in support of core Administration goals. Development and dissemination of relevant materials will facilitate nanotechnology-based commercialization and economic development efforts as well as provide cognizance of the Federal regulations that may apply to such efforts. For example, the Emerging Technologies Interagency Policy Coordination Committee (ETIPC)[23] has released two memoranda to the heads of executive departments and agencies—one on emerging technologies generally and one on nanotechnology specifically—that outline broad principles for regulation and oversight of these technology areas.[24,25] Individual agencies have also issued guidance and rulings as needed and appropriate. Small- and medium-sized businesses are of particular interest for outreach efforts because they may not have the capabilities necessary to easily identify such potentially useful Federal resources and interpret applicable regulations. The primary focus of this objective is to provide the business community and potential entrepreneurs with useful and reliable information in an easy-to-navigate forum for the purpose of increasing awareness of, interest in, and collaboration with federally funded programs designed to support nanotechnology.

2.2. Increase focus on nanotechnology-based commercialization and related support for public–private partnerships.

2.2.1. Sustain successful initiatives and expand the number of public–private partnerships.

2.2.2. Evaluate and disseminate information on best practices to advance commercialization of U.S.-derived nanotechnologies.

2.2.3. Support U.S. industry in the development of technology "roadmaps" or R&D plans in support of public–private partnerships.

2.2.4. Promote development of robust, scalable nanomanufacturing methods with sufficient precision to facilitate commercialization.

The NSET Subcommittee and participating agencies appreciate the importance of collaboration between Federal agencies, academia, and industry, as well as regional, state, and local organizations in facilitating the commercialization of federally funded nanotechnology R&D. Over the years, NNI agencies have interacted with key industry sectors to better understand their technology needs and to develop public–private partnerships and other collaborative mechanisms to address these needs. The NSET Subcommittee has engaged regional, state, and local organizations to explore opportunities

---

[22] www.whitehouse.gov/the-press-office/2011/10/28/presidential-memorandum-accelerating-technology-transfer-and-commerciali

[23] The ETIPC is described more thoroughly in the "Coordination and Assessment" chapter.

[24] www.whitehouse.gov/sites/default/files/microsites/ostp/etipc-memo-3-11-2011.pdf

[25] www.whitehouse.gov/sites/default/files/omb/inforeg/for-agencies/nanotechnology-regulation-and-oversight-principles.pdf

to collaborate to promote business development and remove the barriers to commercialization of NEPs. The NNI will continue these interactions through activities such as workshops, webinars, and other events that provide forums for communication and collaboration, and through outreach activities under the Nanomanufacturing, Industry Liaison, and Innovation (NILI) Working Group. The NSET Subcommittee and participating agencies will also explore the benchmarking of best practices from the commercialization of other advanced technologies to identify innovative approaches that can be applied to facilitate technology transfer and commercialization of NEPs and to share these practices with NNI stakeholders.

Public–Private Partnerships

The Nanoelectronics Research Initiative (NRI) is an exemplar public–private partnership launched in 2005 to collaboratively prioritize and fund university research for the semiconductor industry. NRI, a subsidiary of the Semiconductor Research Corporation, leverages expertise and resources from industry (Semiconductor Industry Association and the following NRI member companies: GLOBALFOUNDRIES, IBM, Intel Corporation, Micron Technology, and Texas Instruments), Federal agencies (NIST and NSF), and State governments (Nebraska, New York, and Texas). More information on NRI is available at www.src.org/program/nri.

NRI supports long-range research toward the discovery of the fundamental building blocks for tomorrow's nanoscale electronics—new devices and circuit architectures for computing—that are viewed as essential to continuing advances in performance of information technology. A key aspect of this program is the close connection between NRI member companies and the student researchers who will become the innovators and leaders of tomorrow's technology industry.

The current NRI program consists of three multidisciplinary, multi-university research centers (the Institute for Nanoelectronics Discovery and Exploration, the Center for NanoFerroic Devices, and the SouthWest Academy of Nanoelectronics) that are jointly supported by NIST and the industry members as well as twelve joint awards with NSF to Nanoscale Interdisciplinary Research Teams in support of the Nanoelectronics for 2020 and Beyond NSI.

Through mechanisms including the NSIs, NNI agencies have collaborated with each other, industry, economic development organizations, universities, and community colleges to tackle the technical barriers to commercialization of NEPs. In their joint memo on R&D priorities for the fiscal year 2015 Federal Budget, the directors of the Office of Management and Budget and the Office of Science and Technology Policy stressed the importance of nanotechnology R&D, particularly that being conducted under the NSIs, to the Administration's advanced manufacturing agenda. NNI agencies will explore ways to strengthen and expand NSI collaborations to advance the state of the art in advanced manufacturing and to facilitate commercialization of advanced technologies.

2.3. Promote broader accessibility and utilization of user facilities, cooperative research centers, and regional initiatives to accelerate the transfer of nanoscale science from lab to market.

2.3.1. Provide economical access to tools and processes, expertise, and training critical to the transition from discovery to advanced prototype development.

2.3.2. Support the establishment of self-sustaining cooperative research centers and regional, state, and local economic development initiatives for nanotechnology commercialization.

NNI agencies have made considerable investments in the development of unique national facilities to support nanotechnology R&D (Goal 3). These investments provide for the development of new capabilities and help to maintain the existing infrastructure needed to support both basic research in nanotechnology and commercialization activities. NNI agencies will continue to support these facilities and provide economical access for industry and university researchers to support both commercialization and research. Further efforts to promote nanotechnology commercialization will be supported through continued efforts to foster government–university–industry consortia and economic development initiatives at the regional, state, and local levels.

2.4. Actively engage in international activities integral to the development and responsible commercialization of nanotechnology-enabled products and processes.

2.4.1. Participate and, where appropriate, lead in the development of international standards for nanotechnology.

2.4.2. Engage in bilateral and multilateral collaborations and cooperative activities to further nanotechnology-related commercialization, innovation, and trade.

2.4.3. Support forums in which U.S. and international stakeholders can exchange technical information and discuss respective market needs, intellectual property rights, and other issues relevant to enabling commercialization.

Significant public and private investments in nanotechnology R&D worldwide have led to the commercialization of an ever-expanding array of NEPs across a variety of industry sectors. At the international level, vibrant and dynamic exchange of information is accompanying the rapid pace of global innovation in nanotechnology and the associated knowledge gains. With supply chains distributed across multiple countries, NNI agencies will continue to engage early and often in international forums that support responsible commercialization and best practices. These include organizations that develop international standards, government-to-government collaborations, and other activities that bring together stakeholders from the United States and around the world.

Many NNI agencies are already active and lead important international activities. Agencies will continue to maintain and strengthen this strategic engagement while balancing budget constraints and mission objectives. NNI agencies will also explore means for leveraging public–private partnerships to maximize the impact of their participation and strengthen ties with the U.S. private sector. NNI agencies' engagements span a wide range of issues, including the development of international standards, exchange of scientific and technical information, and identification of market trends. By participating in a variety of forums and partnerships, NNI agencies will proactively address nanotechnology-related intellectual property rights as well as environmental, health, and safety (EHS); consumer; and societal issues—all of which enable innovation, commercialization, trade, and U.S. leadership in strategic and transformative technologies.

International Symposium on Assessing the Economic Impact of Nanotechnology

Recognizing the importance of linking investments in research to economic and societal development, the NNI partnered with the Organisation for Economic Co-operation and Development's (OECD) Working Party on Nanotechnology to organize a symposium in March of 2012. Methodologies for measuring economic and other impacts of nanotechnology were presented and discussed among the 170 participants from 22 countries with expertise all along the nanotechnology value chain. Several case studies demonstrated where nanotechnology has had a strong impact on specific industries. Associated background papers, presentations, videos of plenary sessions, and a synthesis report are available at www.nano.gov/symposium.

Government Panel Discussion (pictured from left to right): Joseph Molapisi (South Africa); Françoise Roure (France); Naoya Kaneko (Japan); Herbert von Bose (EC); Adalberto Fazzio (Brazil); G. V. Ramaraju (India). Not pictured: Altaf Carim (U.S.)

Goal 3: Develop and sustain educational resources, a skilled workforce, and a dynamic infrastructure and toolset to advance nanotechnology.

Fundamental to the successful development of nanotechnology is the continued development of the infrastructure necessary to support this effort. A substantial investment, strengthened by interagency cooperation and collaboration through the NNI, is needed to develop the talent and facilities necessary to achieve the other NNI goals of advancing a world-class R&D program (Goal 1), fostering the transfer of new technologies into products for commercial and public benefit (Goal 2), and supporting responsible development of nanotechnology (Goal 4).

Nanotechnology is emerging amid a transformative phase in education in the United States when there is a widely recognized need to improve science, technology, engineering, and mathematics (STEM) education. The creation in the United States of a world-leading science and technology workforce can be accelerated by nurturing students' interest in STEM topics. Not only do core STEM concepts underpin nanoscale science and engineering, but the discovery of emergent properties and behaviors at the nanoscale can excite and inspire students to learn about nanotechnology and STEM more broadly. Using traditional teaching methods, hands-on training, informal education programs, and emerging Internet-based education, innovations in nanotechnology can be exploited as vehicles for learning and teaching STEM subjects that some students have traditionally found challenging.

The NNI agencies continue to foster educational programs that develop scientists, engineers, technicians, production workers, and laboratory personnel (including academic students and trainees) through multidisciplinary academic programs, industrial partnerships, and federally funded R&D systems.

Extensive infrastructure capabilities are critical to moving nanotechnology from the research laboratory to production and will continue to be advanced. These capabilities are provided by the centers and user facilities, which broadly support R&D on nanomanufacturing, nanoscale characterization, synthesis, simulation, and modeling.

Goal 3 Objectives

3.1. Sustain outreach and informal education programs in order to inform the public about the opportunities and impacts of nanotechnology.

> 3.1.1. Develop and publish educational and informational materials appropriate for informing the public at large, including students.

> 3.1.2. Establish and maintain mechanisms, such as informational networks, for disseminating and collecting educational materials at all relevant educational levels.

The potential of nanotechnology R&D to result in innovative, cross-cutting discoveries and products should be harnessed to ignite students' enthusiasm for STEM topics and careers. Additionally, NNI agencies will support a mix of established and novel approaches to engage and inform all segments of the public to help them understand the basic principles of nanoscale science. This knowledge will allow the public to appreciate the opportunities presented by nanotechnology as well as its potential impacts on EHS and its ethical, legal, and societal implications (ELSI) (see Goal 4 for more information on EHS and ELSI considerations). Agencies will continue to partner with public and private organizations in order to create informal educational materials such as exhibits, brochures, periodicals, radio and television programming, and other educational mass media.

3.2. Establish and sustain programs that assist in developing and maintaining a skilled nanotechnology workforce.

> 3.2.1. Develop, publish, and disseminate nanotechnology educational materials for educating and training the workforce, appropriate for all relevant education levels, from vocational to professional.

> 3.2.2. Continue to provide opportunities for practical training experience for students in federally supported nanotechnology facilities.

> 3.2.3. Encourage education about the areas of convergence between nanotechnology and other related scientific disciplines, such as biotechnology, information technology, and cognitive science.

The demand for technicians and research scientists to work in nanotechnology-related industries is expected to increase as research on and commercialization of engineered nanomaterials (ENMs) and NEPs continues to mature. Given the interdisciplinary nature of nanotechnology, education programs should provide opportunities for students to acquire the skills to think and collaborate across boundaries in addition to building deep technical knowledge. In order to prepare high school graduates for careers in nanotechnology-related industries, the NNI agencies will work collaboratively to support the development of K–12 education that incorporates problem-based and integrative teaching, where appropriate. With the support of NNI agency-supported centers, colleges and universities have been offering undergraduate minors and majors, teacher training, and postgraduate programs in nanoscale science and engineering. International standards and best practices (e.g., for safe handling of ENMs in the laboratory, as described in Goal 4) will help to inform these developments. Information on nanotechnology and nanoscience-based career opportunities and workforce needs will support the pursuit of this objective. Online resources should be utilized to supplement classroom training and to help disseminate information about careers and formal education programs in nanotechnology.

3.3. Provide, facilitate the sharing of, and sustain the physical R&D infrastructure, notably user facilities and cooperative research centers.

3.3.1. Establish regular mechanisms to determine the current and future infrastructure needs of users and stakeholders of these facilities and centers.

3.3.2. Develop, operate, and sustain advanced tools, infrastructure, and user facilities (including ongoing investment, staffing, and upgrades).

Robust nanotechnology R&D and technical advancement requires the support of state-of-the-art physical infrastructure that is widely accessible. As nanotechnology rapidly advances, shared-use facilities must continuously refresh their equipment to meet the evolving needs of users from industry, academia, and government. Some of the specialized capabilities, equipment, and structures needed for nanoscale science R&D are prohibitively expensive for small enterprises and educational institutions. Sustained and predictable access to a broad range of state-of-the-art instrumentation and facilities for synthesis, processing, fabrication, characterization, modeling, and analysis of nanomaterials and nanosystems, including bio-nanosystems, is needed to achieve this objective. In many cases, no single researcher or even single institution can justify funding the acquisition of and support for all necessary tools, and therefore user facilities that provide access to researchers from multiple sectors serve a critical role. Such facilities enable and accelerate commercialization of R&D by co-locating a broad suite of necessary nanotechnology tools, maintaining and replacing these tools to keep them at the leading edge, and providing expert staff to ensure the most productive use of the tools. The facilities also work to create the next generation of nanoscale fabrication methods and measurement instruments. Finally, the facilities provide a setting for hands-on training of the next generation of nanotechnology researchers and endeavor to create a community of shared ideas by mixing researchers from different disciplines and from different sectors, including industry, academia, and government.

The extensive infrastructure established by the NNI agencies will be upgraded and sustained based on evaluations of the need and capacity requirements. International best practices should be incorporated into the current infrastructure, as appropriate. Extensive publicity and dissemination of information will help to engage nanotechnology researchers and developers, especially from small and medium enterprises, to ensure that this infrastructure is accessible to all and well utilized.

NNI User Facilities: Providing Access to Nanotechnology Expertise and Infrastructure

Several Federal agencies operate nanotechnology user facilities, with access rules, costs, and provisions for proprietary research determined by the individual facilities and their funding agencies.

The National Nanotechnology Infrastructure Network (NNIN) is an integrated, networked partnership of user facilities, supported by the NSF, serving the needs of nanoscale science, engineering, and technology. The NNIN sites provide access to nanofabrication and nanocharacterization tools and operate on a fee-based, open-access model, subject to review for technical feasibility. NSF also supports the Network for Computational Nanotechnology, which provides simulation services and educational material through nanoHUB.org, operating as an open-source, open-access "virtual" user facility.

DOE operates five Nanoscale Science Research Centers (NSRCs), which are available to the research community subject to peer review and merit-based selection. Nonproprietary research projects provide users with access to NSRC and related facilities at no cost. Proprietary research projects are conducted on a cost-recovery basis.

Within DOC, the NIST Center for Nanoscale Science and Technology (CNST) provides rapid access to the tools needed to make and measure nanostructures. These tools are provided to anyone who needs them, both inside and outside NIST, with a particular emphasis on helping industry.

NCI's Nanotechnology Characterization Laboratory (NCL) offers characterization and safety testing of nanoparticles intended for cancer therapies or diagnostics. Following a review process, services are provided at no cost to the submitting investigator.

For more information, see www.nano.gov/userfacilities.

The Center for Nanoscale Science and Technology

Source: National Institute of Standards and Technology

Goal 4: Support responsible development of nanotechnology.

Realization of the potential benefits of nanotechnology for human, social, and economic well-being, and for the environment, requires that responsible development of nanotechnology—assessment and management of potential risks—be integrated into all aspects of the field, from world-class R&D (Goal 1) to commercialization of NEPs (Goal 2). Responsible development is a fundamental component of all three objectives in Goal 3. Research in support of Goal 4 will help address the concerns of many stakeholder groups that are dedicated to protecting humans and the environment.

In 2011, the NNI developed, with input from stakeholders, a nanotechnology-related environmental, health, and safety (nanoEHS) research strategy with a broad, multi-agency perspective.[26] That document fully supports the Goal 4 objectives and details specific research needs in six interrelated and synergistic nanoEHS areas: (1) a *nanomaterial measurement infrastructure* coupled with (2) *predictive modeling and informatics* that provide accurate and reproducible data on (3) *human exposure*, (4) *human health*, and (5) *the environment* essential for science-based (6) *risk assessment and management* of ENMs and NEPs. The NNI agencies, individually and collaboratively, will continue to provide information on progress toward addressing these research needs.

Consideration of life cycle issues of ENMs and NEPs is a key component of all four objectives described below. Advances in these objectives require coordinated efforts involving multidisciplinary, multistakeholder national and international teams.

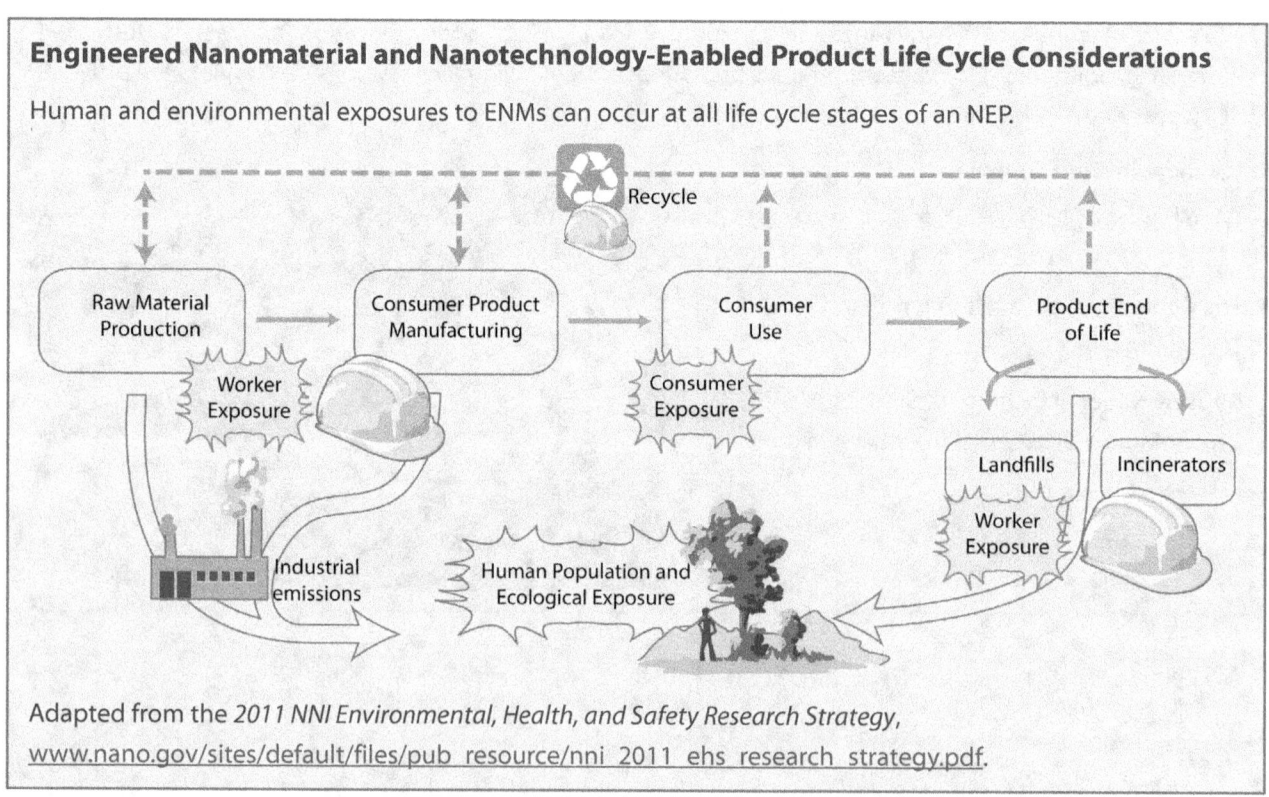

Engineered Nanomaterial and Nanotechnology-Enabled Product Life Cycle Considerations

Human and environmental exposures to ENMs can occur at all life cycle stages of an NEP.

Adapted from the *2011 NNI Environmental, Health, and Safety Research Strategy*, www.nano.gov/sites/default/files/pub_resource/nni_2011_ehs_research_strategy.pdf.

---

[26] www.nano.gov/node/681

Goal 4 Objectives

4.1. Support the creation of a comprehensive knowledge base for evaluation of the potential risks and benefits of nanotechnology to the environment and to human health and safety.

4.1.1. Continue to identify gaps and prioritize needs for relevant knowledge through active stakeholder engagement, including with industry and regional, state, and local initiatives.

4.1.2. Facilitate the development of an informatics-based structure for knowledge sharing that includes a compendium of existing knowledge and mechanisms to incorporate new knowledge.

4.1.3. Promote the development and validation of measurement tools and decision-making models to enable hazard and exposure quantification for human and environmental risk assessment and management.

4.1.4. Participate in international efforts, particularly those aimed at generating best practices and consensus standards.

Science-based risk assessment and management of ENMs and NEPs is predicated on the broad availability of a comprehensive knowledge base that includes validated data, methods, protocols and assays, reference materials and consensus standards, and interpretative and predictive models. Such a knowledge base is also essential for the development of beneficial nanotechnology applications for society and the environment. There is a substantial and rapidly growing body of knowledge on ENM and NEP characterization, hazards, and exposure that needs to be collected, analyzed, organized, and archived in an informatics-based structure to facilitate sharing and use of information. The development of broadly applicable, accessible, and validated measurement tools that enable the generation of accurate and reproducible data remains a high-priority research area. Such tools provide confidence in quantifying hazards, exposure, and ultimately risk, all of which are critical to evaluating the safety of NEPs. Such safety evaluations will accelerate innovation and commercialization of NEPs and support science-based regulatory actions to protect human health and the environment. Decision-making models that are flexible enough to integrate limited amounts of data will accelerate and advance risk assessment and management. The NNI agencies will continue to play a strong participatory and, where appropriate, leading role in international activities to develop consensus standards and in other international activities. Such consensus standards, along with best practices, provide essential guidance to policy-makers and regulators.

Specific research areas for increased emphasis that have been identified collectively by NNI agencies include sustainability (Objective 4.4), high-throughput screening tools, environmental fate and transport, tools for risk assessment and management, dose metrics, and human and environmental health monitoring. Another high-priority need is a library of well-characterized ENMs available for testing by researchers and for use in international interlaboratory studies.

4.2. Create and employ means for timely dissemination, evaluation, and incorporation of relevant EHS knowledge and best practices.

4.2.1. Explore new avenues to engage with a broader group of stakeholders, to communicate NNI research progress, and to share technical information.

4.2.2. Promote multistakeholder activities to evaluate EHS concerns such as human and environmental exposures to ENMs and NEPs.

4.2.3. Participate in coordinated international efforts focused on sharing data, guidance, and best practices for environmental and human risk assessment and management.

NanoEHS is a multidisciplinary research area of importance to a large and diverse group of stakeholders. Thus, it is a challenge to engage, communicate, and share information with stakeholders who have varying concerns and levels of EHS knowledge. Addressing this challenge requires expanded use of modern approaches to disseminate information, such as popular social media tools, and enhanced awareness and new functionality of key websites, notably www.nano.gov. Another approach is enhanced communication of individual NNI agencies' specific research priorities, activities, and interagency collaborations. Advances in the evaluation of specific EHS concerns are enabled by increased participation of diverse stakeholders in existing evaluation activities as well as by initiation of new activities. The NNI agencies will continue to participate in, and where appropriate, lead international efforts focused on sharing information, including safety data, pertinent to risk assessment and management.

4.3. Develop the national capacity to identify, define, and responsibly address concepts and challenges specific to the ethical, legal, and societal implications (ELSI) of nanotechnology.

4.3.1. Support the creation of a comprehensive knowledge base for ELSI and the development of an ELSI infrastructure.

4.3.2. Promote awareness and education of ELSI among relevant stakeholders (including manufacturers, regulators, nongovernmental organizations, workers, and the public).

4.3.3. Foster deliberative interactions, such as public forums, among relevant stakeholders concerning national and global ELSI.

Addressing ELSI in a proactive manner is critical to ensure public trust in nanotechnology and to promote innovation and commercialization of NEPs. The first step in addressing ELSI is to build a comprehensive knowledge base that includes a compendium of ELSI experts, results from societal dimensions research, workshop reports, patents, and best practices to approaching ELSI issues. Such a knowledge base relies on support from an enhanced ELSI infrastructure composed of networks, repositories, and centers for advancing the collection, dissemination, and preservation of societal dimensions research on nanotechnology for both the research community and public audiences. To increase stakeholder awareness and education concerning ELSI issues, appropriate and relevant ELSI knowledge will be disseminated to myriad stakeholders having varying levels of ELSI knowledge. Expanded opportunities and new approaches for deliberative interactions among stakeholder groups, which are numerous and diverse, will be developed and implemented.

4.4. Incorporate sustainability in the responsible development of nanotechnology.

4.4.1. Encourage the development of ENMs that are safer and more sustainable alternatives to materials—nanoscale and otherwise—that are now in use.

4.4.2. Promote the design and development of safe and environmentally benign manufacturing and end-of-life processes for ENMs and NEPs.

4.4.3. Support R&D on nanotechnology with beneficial applications toward human health and the environment.

Sustainability was first illustrated conceptually in 1987 in a two-dimensional Venn diagram as the intersection of society, the economy, and the environment.[27] Materials sustainability, as illustrated below in a more complex, three-dimensional rendition of the concept, encompasses many global challenges of growing societal, economic, and environmental importance: material, water, and air management; green manufacturing; environmental stewardship; and renewable and clean energy sources.[28] Responsible development of nanotechnology must include consideration of these sustainability challenges in the design of manufacturing and end-of-life processes for ENMs and NEPs. New research will be directed at developing ENMs that are more sustainable alternatives to larger-scale materials currently used in myriad processes and products, and at integrating sustainability in the design, development, and manufacture of ENMs and NEPs.

On the other hand, nanotechnology has great potential to address societal, economic, and environmental sustainability needs. Some of the beneficial applications that nanotechnology could provide in support of sustainability are ENMs for more efficient generation and use of energy, water purification, production of food and bio-based industrial and commercial products, and remediation of environmental contaminants. New research will develop these and other nanotechnology applications for widespread positive impact on human health and the environment.

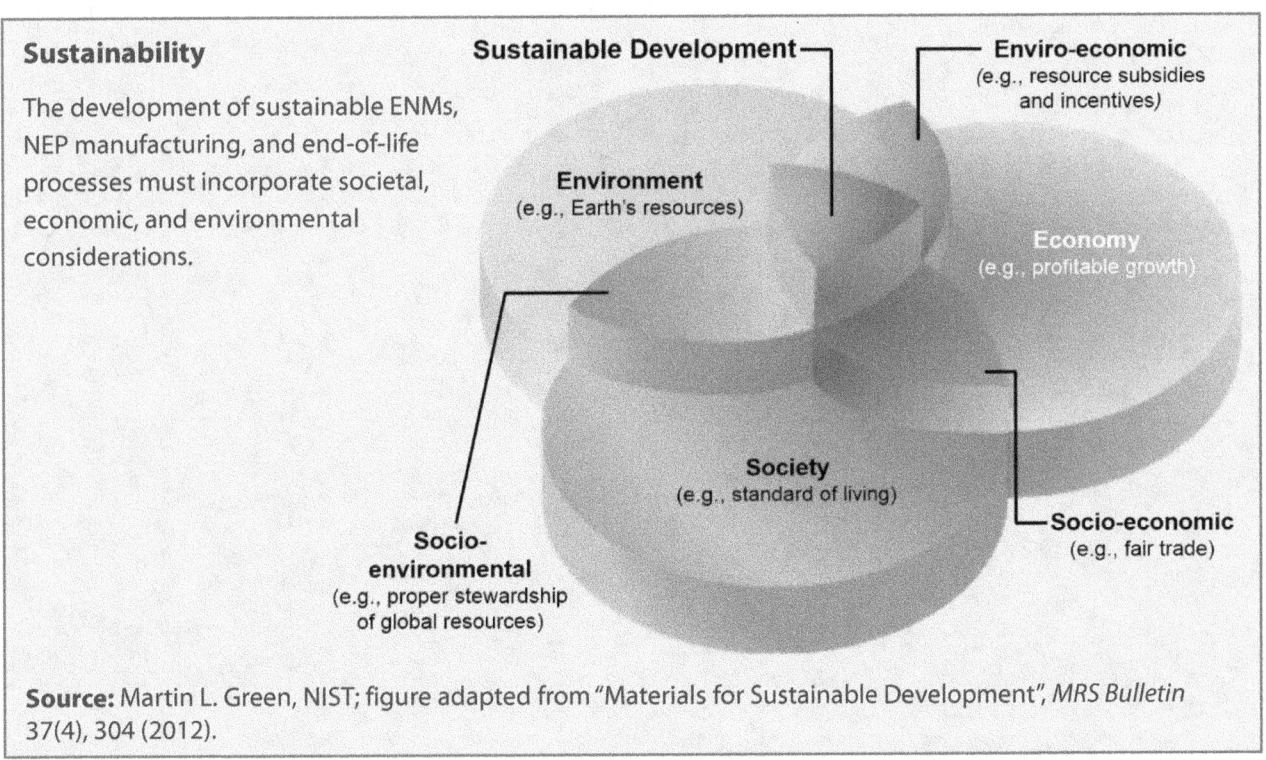

Sustainability

The development of sustainable ENMs, NEP manufacturing, and end-of-life processes must incorporate societal, economic, and environmental considerations.

Sustainable Development

Enviro-economic
(e.g., resource subsidies and incentives)

Environment
(e.g., Earth's resources)

Economy
(e.g., profitable growth)

Society
(e.g., standard of living)

Socio-environmental
(e.g., proper stewardship of global resources)

Socio-economic
(e.g., fair trade)

Source: Martin L. Green, NIST; figure adapted from "Materials for Sustainable Development", *MRS Bulletin* 37(4), 304 (2012).

---

[27] Barbier, E. "The Concept of Sustainable Economic Development." *Environmental Conservation*, 14(2): 101–110. (1987).

[28] Materials for Sustainable Development, *MRS Bulletin*, 37(4), 303-308 (2012).

Program Component Areas

Overview

Program component areas (PCAs) are major subject areas under which are grouped related nanotechnology R&D projects and activities. They provide an organizational framework for categorizing the investments of the NNI agencies. The statutory framework for Federal nanotechnology research and development includes a requirement that PCAs be established and that agencies track the spending associated with each PCA.[29,30] The Nanoscale Science, Engineering, and Technology (NSET) Subcommittee, acting on behalf of the National Science and Technology Council, defines and establishes PCAs such that their planning, coordination, collaboration, investment, and progress are considered critical to achieving the NNI goals and realizing its vision. The PCAs are clearly correlated to the goals and major objectives of the NNI and provide a means to track both NNI agencies' investments and progress. The investments and major changes related to each PCA are reported in the annual NNI Supplement to the President's Budget,[31] augmenting and complementing reporting on technical and other progress associated with the NNI goals and objectives.

The PCAs that were established in the 2004 NNI Strategic Plan and tracked for spending since fiscal year 2006 have served the Initiative well and provided a valuable means to report both investment and progress. The NSET Subcommittee recently concluded that a significant revision of the PCAs was needed to accommodate the maturation of the Initiative, the enhanced emphasis on applications, and the greater participation by agencies and communities that are not focused primarily on R&D. In particular, the agency representatives believe that the Nanotechnology Signature Initiatives (NSIs) have the attributes intended for PCAs—"specific priorities and technical goals that reflect the goals and priorities established for the Program"[32]—and should be formally included for planning, reporting, and tracking purposes. Furthermore, the NSET Subcommittee determined that revision and consolidation of the previous PCAs was needed. The new PCAs are more broadly strategic, fully inclusive, and consistent with Federal research categories. They also eliminate some areas of overlap and redundancy that had proven problematic, while correlating well with the NNI goals and high-level objectives. The new PCAs will be implemented as part of the fiscal year 2015 planning and will be reported on in the *NNI Supplement to the President's 2015 Budget*. Table 2 presents the new PCAs. A comparison and cross-mapping of the new and former PCAs is included in Appendix C.

---

[29] 15 USC § 7501 (c) (2) & (d) (1), (2)
[30] The text that describes each PCA below is as established for formal collection of budget data.
[31] Available at www.nano.gov.
[32] 15 USC § 7501 (c) (2)

Table 2: Program Component Areas Defined for Fiscal Year 2015

1. Nanotechnology Signature Initiatives (NSIs)
Nanotechnology for Solar Energy Collection and Conversion
Sustainable Nanomanufacturing
Nanoelectronics for 2020 and Beyond
Nanotechnology Knowledge Infrastructure (NKI)
Nanotechnology for Sensors and Sensors for Nanotechnology
2. Foundational Research
3. Nanotechnology-Enabled Applications, Devices, and Systems
4. Research Infrastructure and Instrumentation
5. Environment, Health, and Safety

1. Nanotechnology Signature Initiatives[33]

NSIs serve to spotlight topical areas that exhibit particular promise, existing effort, and significant opportunity, and that bridge across multiple Federal agencies. They are intended to be dynamic, with topical areas rotating and evolving over time. This category includes foundational research and nanotechnology-enabled applications, devices, and systems within each NSI, as appropriate. Instrumentation that is specifically developed in support of a confined topical area covered by one of the NSIs is included here, but otherwise, the development or acquisition of more broadly applicable instrumentation (as well as resources devoted to facilities) falls under the separate PCA on Research Infrastructure and Instrumentation. Most research on Environment, Health, and Safety falls within the separate PCA described below, but activities directly pertinent to specific NSIs are reported in this section instead. Note that the NSIs are centered on focused thrust areas as described below, and that activity falling outside these areas is better characterized under other PCAs.

Nanotechnology for Solar Energy Collection and Conversion: Contributing to Energy Solutions for the Future

Enhancing understanding of energy conversion and storage phenomena at the nanoscale, improving nanoscale characterization of electronic properties relevant to solar energy, and utilization of the unique physical phenomena that occur on the nanoscale to help overcome current performance barriers and substantially improve the collection and conversion of solar energy. This NSI has three thrust areas: (1) improving photovoltaic solar electricity generation; (2) improving solar thermal energy generation and conversion; and (3) improving solar-to-fuel conversions.

---

[33] Brief descriptions of the scopes of the current NSIs, as used for consistent collection of budget data, are presented here; more extensive information about the NSIs is provided following the summary PCA descriptions.

Sustainable Nanomanufacturing: Creating the Industries of the Future

Establishing manufacturing technologies for economical and sustainable integration of nanoscale building blocks into complex, large-scale systems by supporting product, tool, and process design informed by and adhering to the overall constraints of safety, sustainability, and scalability. This NSI specifically focuses at this time on high-performance structural carbon-based nanomaterials, optical metamaterials, and cellulosic nanomaterials. The nanomanufacturing NSI has two thrust areas: (1) design of scalable and sustainable nanomaterials, components, devices, and processes; and (2) nanomanufacturing measurement technologies.

Nanoelectronics for 2020 and Beyond

Discovery and use of novel nanoscale fabrication processes and innovative concepts to produce revolutionary materials, devices, systems, and architectures to advance the field of nanoelectronics. The nanoelectronics NSI has five thrust areas: (1) exploring new or alternative "state variables" for computing; (2) merging nanophotonics with nanoelectronics; (3) exploring carbon-based nanoelectronics; (4) exploiting nanoscale processes and phenomena for quantum information science; and (5) expanding the national nanoelectronics research and manufacturing infrastructure network.

Nanotechnology Knowledge Infrastructure (NKI): Enabling National Leadership in Sustainable Design

This NSI has four thrust areas that focus efforts on cooperative interdependent development of (1) a diverse collaborative community; (2) an agile modeling network coupling experimental basic research, modeling, and applications development; (3) a sustainable cyber-toolbox for nanomaterials design; and (4) a robust digital nanotechnology data and information infrastructure.

Nanotechnology for Sensors and Sensors for Nanotechnology: Improving and Protecting Health, Safety, and the Environment

The two thrust areas for this NSI are to: (1) develop and promote adoption of new technologies that employ nanoscale materials and features to overcome technical barriers associated with conventional sensors; and (2) develop methods and devices to detect and identify engineered nanomaterials (ENMs) across their life cycles in order to assess their potential impact on human health and the environment.

2. Foundational Research

Discovery and development of fundamental knowledge pertaining to new phenomena in the physical, biological, and engineering sciences that occur at the nanoscale. Elucidation of scientific and engineering principles related to nanoscale structures, processes, and mechanisms. Research aimed at discovery and synthesis of novel nanoscale and nanostructured materials and at a comprehensive understanding of the properties of nanomaterials ranging across length scales, and including interface interactions. Research directed at identifying and quantifying the broad implications of nanotechnology for society, including social, economic, ethical, and legal implications.

3. Nanotechnology-Enabled Applications, Devices, and Systems

R&D that applies the principles of nanoscale science and engineering to create novel devices and systems, or to improve existing ones. Includes the incorporation of nanoscale or nanostructured materials and the processes required to achieve improved performance or new functionality, including metrology, scale up, manufacturing technology, and nanoscale reference materials and standards. To meet this definition, the enabling science and technology must be at the nanoscale, but the applications, systems, and devices themselves are not restricted to that size.

4. Research Infrastructure and Instrumentation

Establishment and operation of user facilities and networks, acquisition of major instrumentation, workforce development, and other activities that develop, support, or enhance the Nation's physical or human infrastructure for nanoscale science, engineering, and technology. Includes R&D pertaining to the tools needed to advance nanotechnology research and commercialization, including next-generation instrumentation for characterization, measurement, synthesis, and design of materials, structures, devices, and systems. While student support to perform research is captured in other categories, dedicated educational and workforce efforts ranging from curriculum development to advanced training are included here as resources supporting the human infrastructure of the NNI.

5. Environment, Health, and Safety

R&D primarily directed at understanding the environmental, health, and safety impacts of nanotechnology development and corresponding risk assessment, risk management, and methods for risk mitigation.

Nanotechnology Signature Initiatives

In order to accelerate nanotechnology development in key areas of national importance, the Federal agencies participating in the NNI and the Office of Science and Technology Policy (OSTP) identify topics that may be more rapidly advanced through enhanced interagency coordination and focused investment. The NSIs provide a spotlight on these critical areas and define the shared vision of the participating agencies to accelerate the advancement of nanoscale science and technology from research through commercialization.

The NSIs are developed in the context of all four NNI goals and are intended to genuinely affect the agency budget process and dramatically improve ground-level functional coordination between agencies. Inherently interdisciplinary, these R&D efforts benefit greatly from coordinated planning and collaboration. By combining the expertise, capabilities, and resources of appropriate Federal agencies, the NSIs accelerate research, development, or insertion and overcome challenges to application of nanotechnology-enabled products (NEPs). Each contributing agency is committed to coordinating research to achieve the expected outcomes defined in the NSI white papers[34] in order to avoid duplication of effort and to maximize the return on the Nation's research investments.

The NSIs are intended to spotlight areas over a limited time period, depending on the needs of the specific topic. Furthermore, to enable the focused effort required for the success of the NSIs, a limited

---

[34] Available at www.nano.gov/signatureinitiatives.

number will be active at any one time. New topics for consideration may come from stakeholder suggestions, review committee recommendations, evolving Presidential priorities, and/or agency input. Topics of interest will be further developed into proposals by an interagency group represented by at least three agencies and presented to the NSET Subcommittee. The NNI agencies and OSTP select NSI areas based on alignment with national scientific, economic, and environmental priorities; potential impact on the advancement of nanoscale science and technology; and need for enhanced interagency coordination and collaboration (for example, areas that cannot be adequately addressed by a single agency).

The interagency groups supporting each NSI identify its thrust areas (which may evolve as the initiatives develop), R&D targets, and expected near- and long-term outcomes. Participating agency representatives identify programs, resources, and capabilities in their agencies that can contribute to the goals of the NSI and leverage the programs, resources, and capabilities of the other agencies involved in that NSI. Communities of interest among the Federal participants are established through enhanced communication and identify opportunities for joint solicitations or other multi-agency collaboration in support of the NSI goals. The broader community is engaged through webinars, workshops, technical sessions embedded in existing conferences, and other events as appropriate. Such events aim to raise awareness and build a broader community of interest that includes not only the Federal participants, but also those in academia and industry engaged in research, development, and commercialization efforts, such as grantees and other stakeholders. Well-established communities of interest enable leveraging of public and private activities to further accelerate progress and enable sustained endeavors beyond the duration of individual NSIs.

The NSET Subcommittee provides continuous oversight of the NSIs and is provided with a monthly update by the National Nanotechnology Coordination Office (NNCO). The NSIs are highly individual, and the activities depend strongly on the nature of the research area and what is required to advance the specific goals as defined in each white paper. The NSET Subcommittee and OSTP may decide to transition individual NSIs out of the spotlight based on a number of factors that may include the realization of identified goals and outcomes, the emergence of a strong community of interest or public–private partnerships ready to lead coordination efforts, the advancement of the essential science and technology to a stage more appropriately led by the private sector, or in response to evolving national priorities.

The NSET Subcommittee, in collaboration with OSTP, announced three NSI topic areas in February 2010: solar energy, nanomanufacturing, and nanoelectronics. Two additional areas—sensors and informatics—were added in calendar year 2012. The Subcommittee continues to examine other potential areas of nanoscale science and technology that may benefit from similar close coordination. A summary of each of the five NSIs is provided below. Additional information and the NSI white papers are available at www.nano.gov/signatureinitiatives.

Nanotechnology for Solar Energy Collection and Conversion

Collaborating agencies engaged in this NSI include DOC (NIST), DOD, DOE, IC (ODNI), NASA, NSF, and USDA (NIFA).

Solar energy is a promising energy source that has the potential to reduce U.S. dependence on fossil fuels. New innovations and fundamental scientific breakthroughs are required, however, to accelerate the development of solar energy technologies that are economically competitive with conventional fossil fuels. Agencies participating in the NNI have identified a number of physical phenomena where nanotechnology may play a critical role in overcoming current performance barriers to substantially improve the collection and conversion of solar energy.

Certain ENMs and nanostructures have been shown to enhance the absorption of light, increase the conversion of light to electricity, and provide better thermal storage and transport. Nanostructured artificial photosynthetic systems mimicking those found in nature will be important for the conversion of solar energy into chemical fuels. A deeper theoretical understanding of conversion and storage phenomena at the nanoscale, improvements in the nanoscale characterization of electronic properties, and developments that enable economical nanomanufacturing of robust devices will be critical to exploiting the benefits of nanotechnology for solar energy. Product lifetime and reliability of technologies incorporating nanotechnology must also meet or exceed the performance of conventional solar technologies.

The goals of the solar NSI are to enhance understanding of conversion and storage phenomena at the nanoscale, improve nanoscale characterization of electronic properties, and help enable economical nanomanufacturing of robust devices. This NSI currently has three thrust areas: (1) improve photovoltaic solar electricity generation; (2) improve solar thermal energy generation and conversion; and (3) improve solar-to-fuel conversions.

Sustainable Nanomanufacturing: Creating the Industries of the Future

Collaborating agencies engaged in this NSI include DHHS (NIH and NIOSH), DOC (NIST), DOD, DOE, DOL (OSHA), EPA, IC (ODNI), NASA, NSF, and USDA (FS).

This NSI is designed to develop new technologies for the manufacture of advanced materials, devices, and systems based on nanoscale building blocks and components, and for their economical and sustainable integration into complex, large-scale systems. The nanomanufacturing NSI has two thrust areas: (1) design of scalable and sustainable ENMs, components, devices, and processes; and (2) nanomanufacturing measurement technologies. This NSI currently targets three classes of materials—high-performance structural carbon-based nanomaterials, optical metamaterials, and cellulosic nanomaterials—that have the potential for significant economic impact in multiple industry sectors.

The long-term vision for nanomanufacturing is to create flexible, "bottom-up" or "top-down/bottom-up" continuous assembly methods to construct elaborate systems of complex nanodevices. Furthermore, these systems by design will reduce overall environmental and health impacts over their full life cycles. This NSI is developing the foundation for achieving this vision by establishing sustainable industrial-scale manufacturing of functional systems with relatively limited complexity based on ENMs designed to have specific properties. Advances in several areas are required to move beyond laboratory-specific demonstrations: production must be scaled up to a commercially viable throughput and yield; the generation, manipulation, and organization of nanostructures must be accomplished in a precise, controlled, and sustainable manner; and final NEPs must perform to specification over their expected lifetimes without the release of potentially harmful ENMs. The availability of high-throughput, inline metrology to enable closed-loop process control and quality assurance is a critical prerequisite for the development of cost-effective nanomanufacturing. To this end, this NSI is focused directly on the development of inexpensive, rapid, and accurate sensing and measurement techniques.

Nanoelectronics for 2020 and Beyond

Collaborating agencies engaged in this NSI include DOC (NIST), DOD, DOE, IC (ODNI), NASA, and NSF.

The semiconductor industry is a key driver for U.S. and global economic growth and has contributed significantly to the productivity gains experienced over the past several decades. These gains are due, in part, to the continuous miniaturization enabled by advances in materials science, microelectronics design and fabrication, and manufacturing, resulting in ever smaller, faster, and more affordable devices. As length scales of electronic devices approach atomic dimensions, current architectures are reaching physical limits, and new methods for storing and manipulating information must be developed for miniaturization to continue. Further reductions in device dimensions are important to increase processing speed, reduce device switching energy, increase system functionality, and reduce manufacturing cost per bit.

Researchers are pursuing a variety of approaches to provide the scientific bases to overcome the fundamental limitations that exist in the scaling of traditional electronics. Nanoscale science, engineering, and technology will play a significant role and will likely transform the very nature of electronics and the processes by which electronic devices are manufactured. Rapidly reinforcing domestic R&D successes in these arenas could establish a U.S. domestic manufacturing base that will dominate 21st century electronics commerce. The goal of this NSI is to accelerate the discovery and use of novel nanoscale fabrication processes and innovative concepts to produce revolutionary materials, devices, systems, and architectures to advance the field of nanoelectronics.

The nanoelectronics NSI currently has five thrust areas: (1) exploring new or alternative "state variables" for computing; (2) merging nanophotonics with nanoelectronics; (3) exploring carbon-based nanoelectronics; (4) exploiting nanoscale processes and phenomena for quantum information science; and (5) expanding the national nanoelectronics research and manufacturing infrastructure network.

Nanotechnology Knowledge Infrastructure: Enabling National Leadership in Sustainable Design

Collaborating agencies engaged in this NSI include CPSC, DHHS (FDA, NIH, and NIOSH), DOC (NIST), DOD, DOL (OSHA), EPA, NASA, and NSF.

Nanotechnology has a vital role in providing solutions to global challenges by generating and applying new multidisciplinary knowledge of nanoscale phenomena and ENMs, structures, and NEPs. The data underlying this new knowledge base are vast, disconnected, and challenging to integrate into the broad scientific body of knowledge. Nanoinformatics is the science and practice of developing and implementing effective mechanisms for the nanotechnology community to collect, validate, store, share, mine, analyze, model, and apply nanotechnology information. Nanoinformatics is integrated throughout the entire nanotechnology landscape, impacting all aspects of research, development, and application. An improved nanoinformatics infrastructure is critical to the sustainability of our national nanotechnology proficiency by improving the reproducibility and distribution of experimental data and by promoting the development and validation of tools and models to transform data into information and applications. A focused national emphasis on nanoinformatics will provide a strong basis for the rational design of ENMs and NEPs, prioritization of research, and assessment of risk throughout NEP life cycles and across sectors that include energy; environment, health, and safety (EHS); medicine; electronics; transportation; and national security.

The goal of the Nanotechnology Knowledge Infrastructure (NKI) NSI is to provide a community-based, solutions-oriented knowledge infrastructure to accelerate nanotechnology discovery and innovation. This NSI currently has four thrust areas that focus efforts on cooperative interdependent development of: (1) a diverse collaborative community; (2) an agile modeling network for multidisciplinary intellectual collaboration that effectively couples experimental basic research, modeling, and applications development; (3) a sustainable cyber-toolbox to enable effective application of models and knowledge to the design of ENMs; and (4) a robust digital nanotechnology data and information infrastructure to support effective data sharing, collaboration, and innovation across disciplines and applications.

The NKI Signature Initiative and the Materials Genome Initiative[35] have common themes, and through coordination activities, productive and open communication exists at the leadership level and among the agency representatives. Strong collaboration and interaction also exists between the NKI and other related activities, including public–private efforts such as the community coalition of nanotechnology and informatics practitioners steering the Nanoinformatics Roadmap effort[36] and associated workshops in 2010, 2011, and 2012.[37]

Nanotechnology for Sensors and Sensors for Nanotechnology: Improving and Protecting Health, Safety, and the Environment

Collaborating agencies engaged in this NSI include CPSC, DHHS (FDA, NIH, and NIOSH), DOC (NIST), DOD, EPA, NASA, NSF, and USDA (NIFA).

Nanotechnology-enabled sensors are providing new solutions in physical, chemical, and biological sensing that enable increased detection sensitivity, specificity, and multiplexing capability in portable devices for a wide variety of health, safety, and environmental assessments. Compelling drivers for the development of nanosensors include the global distribution of agricultural and manufacturing facilities, creating an urgent need for sensors that can rapidly and reliably detect and identify the source of pollutants, adulterants, pathogens, and other threat agents at any point in the supply chain. The increasing burden of chronic diseases such as cancer and diabetes on the aging U.S. population requires improved sensors to identify early-stage disease and inform disease management. Although several new high-performance nanosensors have demonstrated rapid response and increased sensitivity at reduced size, translation of these devices to the commercial market is impeded by issues of reliability, reproducibility, and robustness.

---

[35] www.whitehouse.gov/mgi
[36] Please refer to www.nanoinformatics.org/nanoinformatics/index.php/Nanoinformatics:Roadmap_2020.
[37] See www.nanoinformatics.org/2010/overview and links therein.

Furthermore, the rise in the use of ENMs in commercial products and industrial applications has increased the need for sensors to detect, measure, and monitor the presence of ENMs potentially released in diverse environments across the entire NEP life cycle, including R&D, manufacturing, use, and disposal or recycling. Currently, there is a very limited suite of sensing devices capable of operating in these complex environments.

The goals of this NSI are to support research on ENM properties and development of supporting technologies that enable next-generation sensing of biological, chemical, and nanoscale materials. This interagency effort coordinates and stimulates creation of the knowledge, tools, and methods necessary to develop and test nanosensors and to track the fate of ENMs in the body, consumer products, the workplace, and the environment.

The current two thrust areas for this NSI are to: (1) develop and promote adoption of new technologies that employ nanoscale materials and features to overcome technical barriers associated with conventional sensors; and (2) develop methods and devices to detect and identify ENMs across their life cycles in order to assess their potential impact on human health and the environment.

Relationship between PCAs and Agency Interests

As for earlier PCAs, the revised PCAs cut across the interests and activities of the NNI agencies and represent areas in which achieving the four NNI goals can be facilitated and expedited through interagency coordination and collaboration. Table 3 shows the relationship between the PCAs and the interests and needs of the agencies. The strength of the relationships correlate broadly with the agencies' R&D investments, and the table also indicates where there are strong correlations between PCAs and agency missions, such as in the regulatory realm. For example, the Department of the Treasury (DOTreas) does not have a dedicated nanotechnology R&D budget but has indicated a primary relationship with PCA 3 and with the NSIs on nanomanufacturing, nanotechnology knowledge infrastructure, and nanosensors. These topics all relate directly to DOTreas's mission through the possibility of enhancing the security of U.S. currency as well as promoting job creation and economic growth.

Successful strategic planning, subsequent execution, and tracking and reporting on the progress and accomplishments associated with the NNI are predicated on a strong and clear connection between the PCAs and the NNI goals and objectives. Table 4 provides a simplified crosswalk between the NNI goals and highest-level objectives and the new PCAs. Note that the strength of the relationship between a given PCA and goal is independent of the relationships of the PCA with the objectives under that goal. For example, PCA 4 (Research Infrastructure and Instrumentation) is of primary importance to the overarching aim of Goal 1 (advance a world-class R&D program) and of secondary importance to each objective in this goal.

One desired outcome in redefining the PCAs is to reduce subjective overlap and redundancy and facilitate agency efforts to categorize individual projects and catalog funding in both planning and execution. The strong connection between the new PCA primary relationships and the goals as illustrated in Table 4 suggests that this desired outcome was achieved. The NSIs are focused and carefully framed to enable consistent and definitive allocation and tracking. The appropriateness and completeness of the PCAs will continue to be assessed by the NSET Subcommittee and will be adjusted as time, priorities, and programs evolve.

Table 3: Relationships between the Program Component Areas and the Missions, Interests, and Needs of NNI Agencies

	1. Nanotechnology Signature Initiatives (NSIs)	Nanotechnology for Solar Energy Collection and Conversion	Sustainable Nanomanufacturing	Nanoelectronics for 2020 and Beyond	Nanotechnology Knowledge Infrastructure	Nanotechnology for Sensors and Sensors for Nanotechnology	2. Foundational Research	3. Nanotechnology-Enabled Applications, Devices, and Systems	4. Research Infrastructure and Instrumentation	5. Environment, Health, and Safety
CPSC	◆				○	○	○	●	●	●
DHHS	◆		●		●	●	●	●	○	●
DHS	◆			●		●	○	●	●	●
DOC	◆	●	●	●	●	○	●	●	●	●
DOD	◆	●	●	●	●	●	●	●	○	○
DOEd							●			○
DOE	◆	●	○	○	○		●	●	●	
DOI							●		●	
DOJ								●		
DOL							●	○		●
DOS							●	○	○	●
DOT							●	●		○
DOTreas	◆	○	●	○	●	●		●		○
EPA	◆		○		●	●	○	●	○	●
IC	◆	●	●	●		●	●	●	○	
NASA	◆	●	●	●	●	●	●	●	○	
NRC								●		
NSF	◆	●	●	●	●	●	●	●	●	●
USDA	◆	●	●		●	●	●	●	○	●
USITC	◆	●	●			●		●		

KEY: ● Primary; ○ Secondary; ◆ Denotes engagement with at least one NSI

Table 4: Relationships of NNI Program Component Areas to NNI Goals and Objectives

	1. Nanotechnology Signature Initiatives (NSIs)	Nanotechnology for Solar Energy Collection and Conversion	Sustainable Nanomanufacturing	Nanoelectronics for 2020 and Beyond	Nanotechnology Knowledge Infrastructure	Nanotechnology for Sensors and Sensors for Nanotechnology	2. Foundational Research	3. Nanotechnology-Enabled Applications, Devices, and Systems	4. Research Infrastructure and Instrumentation	5. Environment, Health, and Safety
GOAL 1	◆	●	●	●	●	●	●	●	●	●
Obj 1.1	◆	●	●	●	●	●	●	●	○	○
Obj 1.2	◆	●	●	●	●	●	●	●	○	●
Obj 1.3	◆	○	○	○	○	○	○	○	○	○
Obj 1.4	◆	●	●	●	●	●	○	○	○	○
GOAL 2	◆	●	●	●	●	●	○	●	●	●
Obj 2.1	◆	●	●	●	●	●	○	●	●	●
Obj 2.2	◆	●	●	●	●	●	○	●	●	○
Obj 2.3	◆	●	●	●	●	●	○	○	●	○
Obj 2.4	◆	●	●	●	●	●	○	●	○	●
GOAL 3	◆	○	●	●	●	○	○	○	●	○
Obj 3.1	◆				○		○	○	●	●
Obj 3.2							○	○	●	○
Obj 3.3	◆	○	●	●	●	○	●	●	●	○
GOAL 4	◆	○	●	○	●	●	●	●	●	●
Obj 4.1	◆		●		●	●	●	●	●	●
Obj 4.2	◆		○		○		○	●	○	●
Obj 4.3	◆				●		●	○	○	●
Obj 4.4	◆	○	●	○	○	○	●	●	○	●

KEY: ● Primary; ○ Secondary; ◆ Denotes relationship with at least one NSI

Coordination and Assessment

The NNI is coordinated, planned, implemented, and reviewed by the Nanoscale Science, Engineering, and Technology (NSET) Subcommittee of the Committee on Technology (CoT) of the National Science and Technology Council (NSTC). Other components of NNI coordination (described more fully below) include thematic NSET working groups, identified coordinators for specific cross-cutting areas, the National Nanotechnology Coordination Office (NNCO), the Executive Office of the President (EOP), and other interagency efforts of national importance. Periodic assessment of the NNI by external advisory bodies provides additional input and guidance to the NNI. The figure on the next page shows the relationships between NNI coordination and assessment bodies. The roles of these entities are further described below.

Nanoscale Science, Engineering, and Technology Subcommittee (NSET)

The NSET Subcommittee was established in 2000 under the NSTC's CoT to coordinate interagency nanotechnology R&D activities. The NNCO was subsequently established as the point of contact on Federal nanotechnology R&D activities and to provide technical and administrative assistance to the NSET Subcommittee. The 21st Century Nanotechnology Research and Development Act of December 2003[38] (hereafter referred to as "the Act") formalized many of the coordination structures that the NSTC had organized, and it established additional mechanisms to ensure that the Federal Government developed sound, informed nanotechnology R&D strategies and policies. This legislation also created the National Nanotechnology Advisory Panel (NNAP), called for a triennial review of the NNI by the National Research Council of the National Academies (NRC/NA), and established additional functions for the NNCO.

The NSET Subcommittee leads the interagency coordination of the Federal Government's nanotechnology R&D enterprise by cooperatively coordinating the research, development, communication, and funding functions of the NNI. The NSET Subcommittee develops the NNI Strategic Plan, prepares the annual NNI Supplement to the President's Budget, and sponsors workshops or other interagency activities that inform the Federal Government's nanotechnology-related decision-making processes. The high-level framework provided by the NNI Strategic Plan establishes goals, objectives, and priorities. The framework also guides and informs the participating agencies in developing their individual nanotechnology R&D implementation plans. The Subcommittee member agencies invest across all of the critical areas needed to support the development and utilization of nanotechnology. Further, the Subcommittee interacts with pertinent academic, industry, state, local government, and other Federal government groups, and with international organizations. Each agency participating in the NNI is represented on the NSET Subcommittee; a list of those agencies is given at the front of this report. A co-chair from the Office of Science and Technology Policy (OSTP) and a co-chair from an NNI agency lead the NSET Subcommittee, which meets at least six times each year.

---

[38] Pub. L. No. 108-153, § 7501, 117 Stat. 1923 (2003).

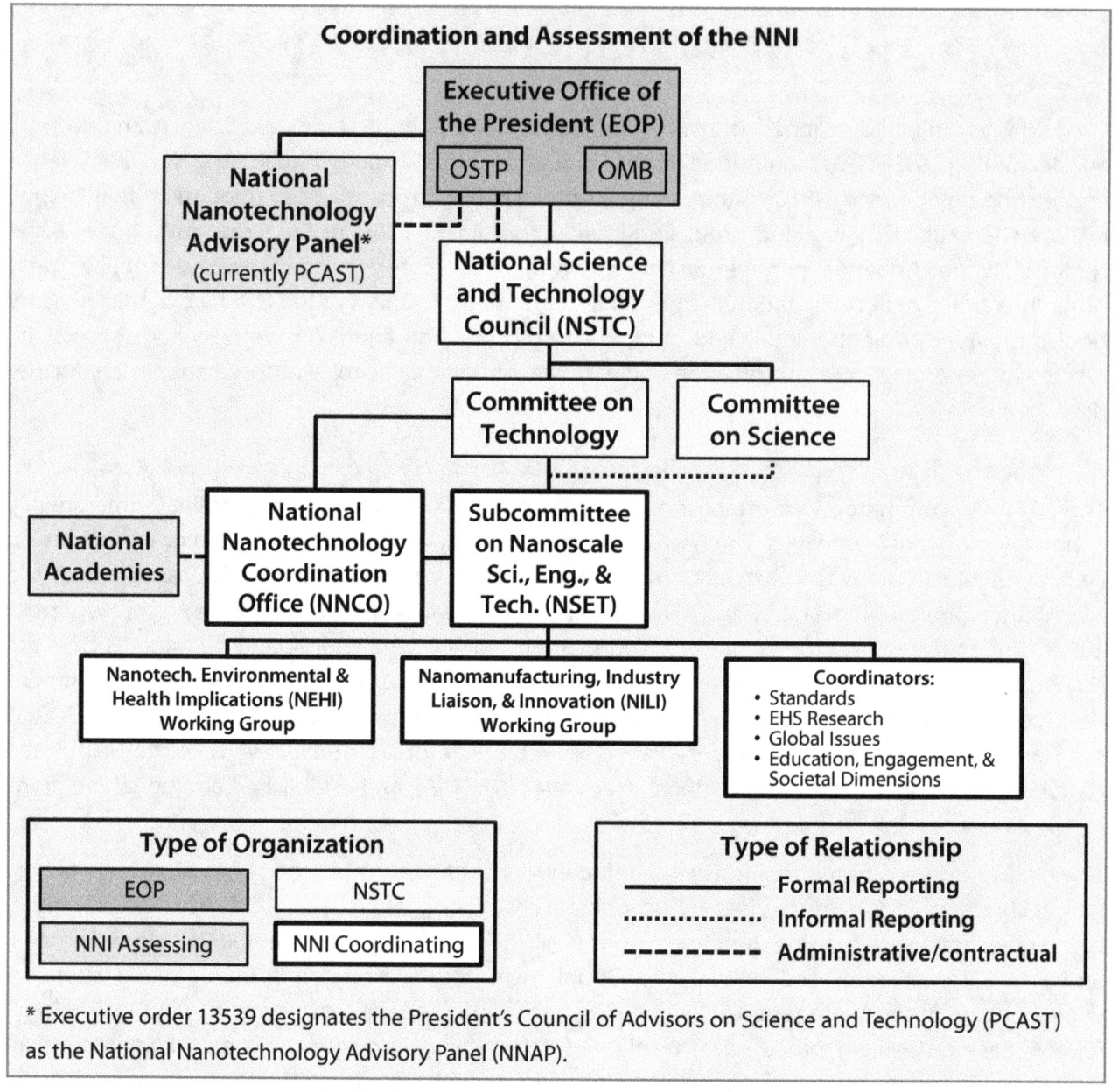

Coordination and Assessment of the NNI

Working Groups of the NSET Subcommittee

The NSET Subcommittee has chartered subsidiary working groups[39] to provide a structure to improve the effectiveness and productivity of the Subcommittee and its participating agencies in areas that will benefit from focused interagency attention and activity. The current working groups are the Nanotechnology Environmental and Health Implications (NEHI) Working Group and the Nanomanufacturing, Industry Liaison, and Innovation (NILI) Working Group. The NSET Subcommittee periodically reviews the need for existing or new working groups in terms of focus, intended participation, and scope, as reflected in the groups' charters.

---

[39] The latest information on each of the NSET working groups is at www.nano.gov/about-nni/working-groups.

Nanotechnology Environmental and Health Implications (NEHI) Working Group

Nanotechnology has the potential to significantly transform society in many key areas including new materials, processes, and products. In order to fully realize the promise of nanotechnology, Federal agencies support research to understand the environmental, health, and safety (EHS) implications of nanotechnology and provide guidance on the safety of nanomaterials across the product life cycle. The NSET Subcommittee's NEHI Working Group provides a forum for focused interagency collaborations on EHS and leadership in establishing the national nanotechnology EHS research agenda, in addition to communicating EHS information among NNI agencies and to the public. The combined efforts of the nanotechnology R&D community, public health advocacy groups, and the public are required to fully address EHS research priorities and strengthen the scientific foundation of risk assessment and risk management of nanotechnology. NEHI provides the nexus, as appropriate, for interactions between agencies and these diverse communities. The sum of these interactions and activities enhances the value of NNI efforts and provides a collaborative approach to examining public health and environmental concerns about nanomaterials. NEHI member agencies include those with direct responsibilities for public, workplace, and environmental safety, and agencies involved in science, education, and policy.

Nanomanufacturing, Industry Liaison, and Innovation (NILI) Working Group

A sustained commitment to nanotechnology-based innovation is key to realizing the NNI vision. This commitment is brought about by cooperation, dialogue, and partnerships among all the stakeholders in the nanotechnology innovation ecosystem. The NSET Subcommittee's NILI Working Group coordinates activities in this area. NILI promotes and facilitates exchange of information and collaborations among Federal agencies, academia, industry, and regional, state, and local (RSL) organizations to build U.S. leadership in nanotechnology-enabled products and commercialization through activities such as developing and maintaining databases of nanotechnology-related technology transfers, nanotechnology standards, and Federal regulations across agencies. More information on these resources is available at www.nano.gov/NILI. NILI periodically organizes workshops that bring together RSL stakeholders. In particular, NILI seeks to help the NNI agencies organize coherent support structures and effective or best technology transfer practices, making good use of the expertise of industry-initiated liaison groups. These liaison groups are a conduit for partnerships between the NNI agencies and industry sectors and generally represent particular industries (e.g., electronics, chemicals, and forest products). A significant component of supporting the innovation process is fostering development of standard nanotechnology reference materials, terminology, and measurement and characterization methods. As with the other NSET Subcommittee working groups, communication, outreach, and engagement activities are significant foci of the NILI Working Group.

Coordinator Functions

Based on a 2010 recommendation from the President's Council of Advisors on Science and Technology (PCAST),[40] the NNI designates coordinators in cross-cutting topical areas to track developments, lead in organizing activities, report periodically to the NSET Subcommittee, and serve as central points of

---

[40] www.whitehouse.gov/sites/default/files/microsites/ostp/pcast-nano-report.pdf

contact for NNI information in the corresponding areas. These coordinators work with NNI agencies to identify priorities and emerging opportunities and to strengthen interagency coordination on these critical topics. The individuals serving in these positions are appointed from either the NNCO or an NNI agency. Initially two coordinators were identified:

- Coordinator for Standards Development.
- Coordinator for Environmental, Health, and Safety Research.

The coordinator mechanism serves as an agile and efficient means to monitor and coordinate agency interests and interactions in these areas. As a result, two additional positions of this type have been established:

- Coordinator for Global Issues.
- Coordinator for Education, Engagement, and Societal Dimensions.

The Coordinator for Global Issues assumes some of the functions of the previous Global Issues in Nanotechnology (GIN) Working Group. This coordinator will work in close concert with other bodies, including NSET's NEHI Working Group (considering the strong global interest in EHS research); the NSTC Subcommittee on Topics in International Science, Technology, and Innovation; and the nanotechnology subgroup of the Emerging Technologies Interagency Policy Coordination Committee, which engages in numerous international dialogues that involve nanotechnology, particularly with respect to regulatory aspects. The Coordinator for Education, Engagement, and Societal Dimensions consolidates related activities in the areas of formal and informal education, public engagement and communication, and societal dimensions, including the ethical, legal, and societal implications of nanotechnology. This involves some functions of the previous Nanotechnology Public Engagement and Communications (NPEC) Working Group, such as preparation for and organization of public outreach activities and other events.

The transition of international interactions and public engagement activities from a working group structure to a coordinator function provides an opportunity to renew and concentrate efforts in these areas. Groups of interested NSET representatives serve as a resource and information distribution channel for the corresponding coordinators and may convene informally for meetings or other events on an occasional basis. Additional coordinators may be appointed as needed.

National Nanotechnology Coordination Office (NNCO)

The NNCO serves as a pivotal locus for the NNI by providing technical and administrative support for the NSET Subcommittee; serving as a central point of contact for Federal nanotechnology R&D activities, including NSET working groups; and performing public outreach and engagement on behalf of the NNI.

The NNCO organizes meetings of the NSET Subcommittee and its working groups, providing staff members to serve as central points of contact and to record and maintain minutes of the meetings. The NNCO also organizes NNI-sponsored workshops and prepares and publishes reports of those workshops. It coordinates the preparation and publication of NNI interagency planning, budget, and assessment documents, such as the annual NNI Supplement to the President's Budget. The NNCO serves as a Congressional liaison by coordinating the development of information on the NNI and its activities for Congress when requested.

The NNCO produces and distributes information for the general public, including brochures, workshop reports, nanotechnology-related news, educational resources, funding opportunities, and other information, all of which are made available on the NNI website, www.nano.gov. This website, which is designed, organized, and maintained by the NNCO, also provides information about recent developments in nanotechnology and NNI activities. The NNCO communications effort is strengthened by relationships between NNCO staff and key press contacts and public information officers at NNI agencies. NNCO staff members prepare and deliver presentations and lectures on NNI activities at professional society meetings and at a wide variety of public venues. The NNCO will continue to organize diverse public input and outreach activities; future examples may include interactive web dialogues, citizen panels, workshops, and other educational events.

Contributions from the NNI agencies fund the NNCO. The White House Chair of the NSTC Committee on Technology appoints the NNCO Director and Deputy Director in consultation with the co-chairs of the NSET Subcommittee.

Executive Office of the President (EOP)

Representatives from EOP participate in NNI activities to ensure that implementation of the NNI is coordinated and consistent with Government-wide priorities. The primary points of interaction are OSTP and the Office of Management and Budget (OMB).

OSTP is responsible for advising the EOP on matters relating to science and technology and supports coordination of interagency science and technology activities. OSTP administers the NSTC, and the OSTP representative to the NSET Subcommittee is a co-chair of the Subcommittee. This arrangement provides EOP-level input on and support for various NNI activities.

OMB is responsible for coordinating with the NNI agency budget offices to establish the nanotechnology R&D budget for planning and tracking purposes. Each year, OMB collects budget information regarding the total Federal investment in nanotechnology R&D as well as information about agency investments within each program component area.

Related Interagency Activities

The NNI is committed to leveraging other interagency efforts that are synergistic with nanotechnology. These related activities include interagency policy coordination committees, other NSTC subcommittees, and other national initiatives. The Emerging Technologies Interagency Policy Coordination Committee was established to better coordinate cross-cutting policy issues (such as regulatory approaches) associated with emerging technologies among Federal agencies, and nanotechnology issues are specifically addressed by a designated subgroup. Two other NSTC bodies with nanotechnology components are the Advanced Manufacturing Subcommittee and the Materials Genome Initiative Subcommittee; the NNI has ongoing interactions with both of them. The Brain Research through Advancing Innovative Neurotechnologies (BRAIN) Initiative is a developing effort in which nanotechnology is expected to have a significant enabling role.

Assessment

The Act calls for periodic assessment of the NNI through annual interagency reporting and through review by external advisory bodies. The annual interagency analysis of progress called for in the Act is provided in the NNI Supplement to the President's Budget,[41] which also serves as the NNI annual report called for in the Act. Specifically, progress toward achieving NNI goals and priorities is analyzed in terms of (1) investments categorized by program component area (PCA), including cross-cutting interagency activities coordinated through the NSET Subcommittee, and (2) activities relating to the four NNI goals, including individual agency activities as well as activities coordinated with other agencies and institutions, including international interactions.

Review by outside advisory groups is vital to keeping NNI efforts focused and balanced, and the Act established two mechanisms for such review. First, the Act calls for the President to establish a National Nanotechnology Advisory Panel to advise the President and the NSTC on matters relating to the NNI. The Act specifically calls for the NNAP to assess the Federal nanotechnology R&D program at least once every two years. Executive Order 13539 (2010) designates PCAST as the NNAP. The members of PCAST are senior representatives from industry and academic research institutions who have extensive experience in managing large science and technology organizations. Second, the Act calls for the NNCO Director to make arrangements for NRC/NA to review the NNI every third year. NRC/NA panels for the NNI reviews are typically comprised of a broad cross-section of technical experts with knowledge specifically related to nanotechnology. The NRC/NA provides independent science, technology, and health policy advice to the Federal Government. It is the principal operating agency of the National Academies in providing services to the Federal Government, the public, and the scientific and engineering communities.

The first assessment by PCAST in its role as the NNAP was released in May 2005, and the first NRC/NA review under the Act was completed in November 2006. Subsequent reviews from PCAST were completed in April 2008, March 2010, and April 2012, and the NRC/NA delivered reports in December 2009 and April 2013. The perspectives of these two bodies, and their assessments, are complementary, and the NNI has benefited from their diverse inputs into the planning and evaluation process. The resulting recommendations have led to specific actions and focused attention in areas that were highlighted by both groups, including research on environmental, health, and safety aspects of nanotechnology; quantitative metrics to assess the progress of the Initiative; and expanded efforts to improve education and workforce preparation, as well as program management.

---

[41] Available at www.nano.gov.

Concluding Remarks

This fourth NNI Strategic Plan, developed by the Nanoscale, Science, Engineering, and Technology (NSET) Subcommittee, addresses evolving scientific, technological, and societal priorities, as well as the needs of the broader nanotechnology community. The same NNI foundational principles and practices on which the three earlier strategic plans were built are embodied in this consensus plan:

- A common vision—*a future in which the ability to understand and control matter at the nanoscale leads to a revolution in technology and industry that benefits society.*
- A framework that provides context for NNI agencies in the formulation of their intramural and extramural research portfolios and allocation of their resources in support of their agency-specific missions.
- Collective and concerted efforts of the NNI agencies to achieve the four goals through the stated objectives, via individual agency and multi-agency collaborative initiatives and activities.
- Continuous needs assessments via outreach to myriad stakeholders by means ranging from informal interactions to webinars and stakeholder workshops.
- Open, transparent communication with the general public regarding the benefits and potential risks of nanotechnology to human health and the environment.
- Strong, proactive engagement with international organizations.

Several aspects of this current strategic plan differ significantly from the prior plans. The program component areas (PCAs) were revised to better represent the current state of nanotechnology; the revisions addressed, among other things, substantial advances in applications and commercialization, expanded interagency collaborations, and broader participation of agencies in non-R&D activities. Finally, the revised PCA descriptions are better aligned with the goals and objectives of the current plan. Some of the objectives were changed to reflect nanotechnology advances and evolving stakeholder needs and to hone the language to facilitate clearer communication and comprehension of the objectives. Improved consistency among the goals was achieved by assigning sub-objectives to each objective and by making the level of specificity of the text for the objectives more uniform.

In the past three years, extensive progress has been made by the NNI agencies in addressing the goals and associated objectives in the 2011 NNI Strategic Plan, as detailed in the agency updates available in the annual NNI Supplement to the President's Budget.[42] Several notable achievements illustrate such progress. The three Nanotechnology Signature Initiatives (NSIs) initiated in 2010 are models of successful interagency collaborations that leverage the strengths, resources, and investments of the NNI agencies. Two new NSIs were established in 2012 that cut across many nanotechnology application areas and are aligned with the plans and activities of the agencies participating in each of these NSIs. To foster technology transfer and business creation, the NNI held a Regional, State, and Local Initiatives in Nanotechnology Workshop in 2012 to discuss Federal resources available to regional, state, and local (RSLs) organizations, as well as RSL best practices. The functionality and

---

[42] Available at www.nano.gov.

content of the NNI website www.nano.gov have been greatly expanded to establish a robust hub for nanotechnology information dissemination aimed at a multitude of stakeholder groups. For example, there are comprehensive webpages devoted to addressing common concerns of nanotechnology start-up companies and providing education and training resources for K–12 students and teachers, as well as compilations of educational institutions with nanotechnology-focused programs at the associate, bachelor, and doctoral levels. The website contains over 150 publications and resources on scientific, educational, and societal dimensions workshops; current and historical NNI budget documents; and the research strategies of individual NNI agencies. Interagency collaborations are widespread and varied in nature; since the launch of the Initiative, its annual budget supplements and other documents have identified well over a hundred concrete efforts involving multiple agency collaboration, including joint and parallel solicitations, interagency agreements, memoranda of understanding, co-sponsored workshops, and jointly operated facilities.

Since the inception of the NNI in 2000, nanotechnology has been increasingly relied upon across broad areas of national importance, enabling revolutionary advances in diverse areas such as cancer treatment, renewable energy, and information processing. Building on these advances and future developments, it is expected that new nanotechnology-enabled applications, products, and systems will emerge with novel and improved functionality and performance. These innovations are enabled by ongoing support from NNI agencies and by the insight and expertise of the entire stakeholder community, including academic researchers, industry representatives, and the public. The NNI and its agencies are committed to sustaining and enhancing the role of the Federal Government in assuring that all aspects of nanotechnology—R&D, commercialization, infrastructure (education, workforce, and research facilities), and responsible development—are strengthened to benefit society, the U.S. economy, and international competitiveness.

Appendix A. External Assessment and Stakeholder Input

As referenced throughout this plan, multiple independent, external sources provided the NNI with advice and recommendations during the creation of this document. In contrast to the other public NNI-sponsored workshops held in 2011–2013 spanning a variety of nanotechnology themes, the resources below specifically targeted the development of this document.

External Assessment Reports

The President's Council of Advisors on Science and Technology performed the fourth assessment of the NNI, releasing the *Report to the President and Congress on the Fourth Assessment of the National Nanotechnology Initiative*[43] on April 27, 2012, and the National Research Council released the *Triennial Review of the National Nanotechnology Initiative*[44] on April 23, 2013. Both reports are largely supportive of the NNI and contain a number of specific recommendations that the Nanoscale Science, Engineering, and Technology (NSET) Subcommittee has considered and incorporated where practical and appropriate in its planning activities and in drafting this strategic plan.

2013 NNI Strategic Planning Stakeholder Workshop, June 2013

To strengthen the development of this strategic plan, the NNI held the *2013 NNI Strategic Planning Stakeholder Workshop* on June 11–12, 2013, in Washington, DC, to solicit public input. Members of the nanotechnology stakeholder community who attended the workshop included those already familiar with the field of nanotechnology and the NNI as well as those new to nanoscale science, engineering, and technology; they comprised members of the public; industry representatives; researchers; members of Federal, state, and local governments and regional initiatives; and representatives of nongovernmental organizations. Their input was invaluable in the development of the 2014 NNI Strategic Plan. Recommendations from the community have been carefully considered in creating the objectives found in this document. A summary of the workshop plenary presentations and breakout sessions is available in Appendix B.

Public Comment on Draft Strategic Plan, November 2013

A draft of the NNI Strategic Plan was released for a thirty-day public comment period from November 19 to December 18, 2013. This was announced in the Federal Register and on www.nano.gov. Responses and recommendations were received from the broad stakeholder community, including academic researchers and administrators, industry representatives, and nongovernmental organizations. All responses are available for public inspection at www.nano.gov/2014strategy and were considered by the NSET Subcommittee in the final preparation of this plan.

---

[43] www.whitehouse.gov/sites/default/files/microsites/ostp/PCAST_2012_Nanotechnology_FINAL.pdf
[44] www.nap.edu/catalog.php?record_id=18271

Appendix B. 2013 NNI Strategic Planning Stakeholder Workshop Summary

The *2013 NNI Strategic Planning Stakeholder Workshop* was held on June 11–12, 2013, in Washington, DC. The goal of the workshop was to obtain input from stakeholders regarding revisions to the NNI Strategic Plan that were proposed at the workshop. The recommendations of this one-and-a-half day workshop informed the development of the 2014 NNI Strategic Plan.

The workshop was attended by approximately 120 participants from a variety of backgrounds, including government; academia; industry; regional, state, and local initiatives; and nongovernmental organizations. In addition, approximately 150 people viewed the live webcast of the plenary sessions.

More information about the workshop, including links to the agenda, presentation slides, a participant list, and videos of the plenary presentations, is available at www.nano.gov/stakeholderworkshop.

Plenary Sessions

Plenary presentations were designed to give a broad overview of the nanotechnology landscape, including major challenges and opportunities.

Welcome, NNI Overview, & Charge to Participants

Altaf Carim, Office of Science and Technology Policy, Executive Office of the President

Dr. Carim opened the workshop by welcoming all of the participants. He gave a broad overview of the NNI, remarking that the Initiative is not a distinct funding program. Instead, it represents a priority area for Government investment and activity.

The NNI Strategic Plan is updated triennially, and Dr. Carim described how the document has evolved since it was first published in 2004. Most notably, objectives have been added to each of the four major goals, and the program component areas have been introduced and revised.

The Nanotechnology Signature Initiatives (NSIs) represent topical priorities of national importance that may be more rapidly advanced through focused interagency coordination. Observing that the NNI is broad, Dr. Carim stated that the NSIs are intended to be very specific. For example, the Sustainable Nanomanufacturing NSI does not encompass all nanomanufacturing. Rather, it focuses on three particular materials: carbon-based materials, optical metamaterials, and cellulosic materials. The NSIs are intended to be dynamic, with topics transitioning in and out of the spotlight as their goals are met and as national priorities evolve.

Dr. Carim asked the meeting participants to provide input on changes in the community and in the science since the publication of the 2011 NNI Strategic Plan, new opportunities and challenges, areas of emphasis and priority, and NNI approaches and activities. Further, he invited attendees to consider the relationships between the goals and objectives and the revised program component areas as well as the NSIs.

Synergies with Other Federal Initiatives

Thomas Kalil, Office of Science and Technology Policy, Executive Office of the President

Mr. Kalil presented an overview of various science and technology initiatives in the Federal Government and how these activities build on and reinforce the NNI. He noted that nanotechnology has the potential to address many of the Obama Administration's priorities, including economic development, clean energy technologies, and improved medical care.

President Obama announced the Materials Genome Initiative (MGI) in 2011 to reduce the time from discovery to high-volume manufacturing and to make the process of developing new materials more predictive. The goal of the MGI is to develop a "materials innovation infrastructure," including computational and experimental tools, digital data, and collaborative networks. Mr. Kalil remarked that there is a high level of overlap between the MGI and the NNI.

The effort to identify and pursue grand challenges is a key element of President Obama's strategy for American innovation. Mr. Kalil cited the EV Everywhere and SunShot programs at the Department of Energy as potential challenges in which nanotechnology could play a role. He further stated that the idea for the Brain Research through Advancing Innovative Neurotechnologies (BRAIN) Initiative, which was launched in 2013, grew out of an interdisciplinary workshop with nanoscientists in attendance, highlighting the need to support interactions at the intersections of disciplines.

Acknowledging that the Obama Administration enthusiastically supports fundamental research, Mr. Kalil mentioned the cross-cutting desire to more efficiently move ideas from the lab to the market. This is particularly important in areas that are expensive and take a long time to develop, because angel and venture investors don't find these investments attractive. To this end, Mr. Kalil listed several promising commercialization models for nanotechnology:

- Identification of areas where the Government can serve as an early adopter.
- Collaborations between industry and academia, funded by industry and Government. These collaborations address industrial needs that are beyond industrial timelines.
- Identification of areas where Government initiatives support advanced manufacturing and translational research at high technology readiness levels.
- Collaborations between Government and large companies that have corporate venture capital arms and that are prepared to make strategic nanotechnology-based investments.

Mr. Kalil closed his talk by recommending a retrospective look at various sectors impacted by nanotechnology to see how the NNI has met its goals and to identify where there is room for improvement.

Bridging Technologies

Paul Braun, University of Illinois at Urbana-Champaign

The central thesis of Prof. Braun's talk was that scientists and engineers need to bridge nanoscience with macroscale systems to realize the full potential of nanotechnology. He gave several examples, such as carbon black, clay, and pigments, of pervasive materials with nanoscale elements. The common attribute of these systems is that they are all commodities.

Prof. Braun pointed out that many of the high-profile nanotechnology-enabled products (NEPs) on the market involve two-dimensional thin films in microelectronics, but nanotechnology can be more powerful if it is used in three-dimensional systems. He discussed how a paradigm shift is needed in product development; otherwise, the steady rate of progress in established products will surpass the incremental improvements from nanotechnology due to the long development timelines.

Prof. Braun used three case studies to illustrate how nanotechnology can be bridged with macroscopic systems. The first example was the production of low-cost, large-area periodic structures with multibeam holography. These three-dimensional photonic crystals were assembled with a common two-dimensional semiconductor to produce a light-emitting diode (LED). The second example cited by Prof. Braun was the use of nanotechnology to make a layered clay material that acts as a thermal insulator. Based on the fact that thermal conductivity decreases as the number of surfaces increases, the Braun research group made materials with ultralow thermal conductivity by including approximately one interface per nanometer. The third example of bridging between the nano- and macroscales was lithium-ion batteries. A typical battery is already inherently nanostructured, but to improve the efficiency of these devices, the nanostructures need to be fabricated in a highly controlled and affordable way. Prof. Braun described how his research lab is using self-assembly to address this issue. He concluded by saying that the goal is to make nanotechnology so commonplace that it is considered boring.

Commercializing Nanotechnology

Christopher Schuh, Massachusetts Institute of Technology

Prof. Schuh began by saying that the only way research can truly connect to society is through products introduced to the market. However, all products will have to go through a nonlinear gauntlet of challenges that present opportunities for redirection. Prof. Schuh presented six case studies of nanotechnology commercialization that illustrate successful course corrections.

The first three examples of course correction all came during the implementation phase when the scientific idea was developed, scaled up, and integrated into a product. The targeted application evolved from low-power batteries to high-power batteries as development of nanospinels proceeded. The synthetic process for making silver nanowires for use in touch screens was completely transformed during scale-up. The targeted implementation of quantum dot LEDs was modified during the integration phase to provide a drop-in replacement for current technologies. Prof. Schuh noted that the integration stage presents a significant opportunity for adjustment because nanotechnology is often integrated into larger products. However, this means that infrastructure and economic interests bias technology toward incremental changes.

The next two case studies illustrated how course corrections were made after the products interacted with the market. Prof. Schuh described how developers discovered an opportunity to detect common fungal infections and reduce mortality rates after introducing magnetite nanoparticles to the market for a different application. Corrosion- and impact-resistant coatings were slowly adopted in products such as machining parts because they created a premium product in a commodity space. When the coatings were used in electronics, however, they were more successful because chip manufacturers were able to use less coating and less gold, which added value for the customer.

The final example presented by Prof. Schuh was that of strained silicon in computing, which is arguably the most pervasive NEP on the market. However, it had a circuitous path through many target applications and development venues before it was successfully implemented. Now it is integrated into every newly produced computer chip.

Infrastructure Needs

Julia Phillips, Sandia National Laboratories

Dr. Phillips began her talk with an overview of current nanotechnology infrastructure capabilities. Scientists can observe a diverse set of nanostructures and real-time structural changes. They can also create, assemble, and manipulate a wide range of nanostructures, but this is often done one structure at a time. A primary challenge in the future will be consistently creating identical structures in high volumes. Dr. Phillips suggested that combinatorial methods should be used to explore the vast territory of potential new materials. As nanotechnology matures, techniques will continue to evolve to address more complex nanomaterial systems.

Dr. Phillips next outlined six opportunities to sustain and improve nanotechnology infrastructure:

- Fast, cheap, and robust methods for *nanomanufacturing*, including tools that measure effects on the environment, health, and safety. Dr. Phillips further suggested strengthening the connection between fundamental science and commercialization.
- *Nanometrology* to characterize increasingly complicated architectures and systems. Two particularly important challenges are developing techniques to assess quality against standard materials and to analyze composition and properties at the same site.
- Recapitalization to maintain state-of-the-art *physical infrastructure*. Innovative approaches to integrating across the value chain should be considered. There is also a need for enhanced coordination and specialization across the national user facilities.
- Physical and virtual *access to facilities and infrastructure*. This is particularly important for facilities with unique or expensive equipment. Dr. Phillips also mentioned that a spectrum of access models need to be available to users based on their needs.
- *Approaches to complexity* to address issues such as identifying relevant variables in multiscale integrated nanostructures and big data sets. Possible approaches include visualization approaches to data analysis and simplifying overly complicated subjects.
- A *qualified talent pool*. It is important to instill interdisciplinary fluency as well as a deep technical expertise in nanotechnology researchers. Dr. Phillips also emphasized the need to foster nanotechnology literacy in the general public.

International Challenges and Opportunities

Shaun Clancy, Evonik Corporation

Dr. Clancy outlined four international challenges in nanotechnology as well as several groups that are working to address these issues. *Terminology* plays a critical role in how information is exchanged. A number of groups are developing nanotechnology terminology, including Technical Committee 229 (TC 229) of the International Organization for Standardization (ISO). The next challenge is *safety*, which is a primary concern across the international community. Dr. Clancy outlined several activities on this topic, such as inhalation research in the United States and work in Germany on the translocation of engineered nanomaterials (ENMs) within organisms. Another challenge is *regulation*. Dr. Clancy stated that industry recognizes the importance of regulations that provide appropriate oversight without becoming too burdensome. The final challenge is *international regulatory cooperation*. In particular, Dr. Clancy described the research program within the Working Party on Manufactured Nanomaterials (WPMN) of the Organisation for Economic Co-operation and Development (OECD). The goal is to group ENMs into families such that each material does not have to be considered individually.

In addition to the activities outlined above, Dr. Clancy described four international opportunities, one of which is *transnational activities* to facilitate the development of nanotechnology. For example, the International Alliance for NanoEHS Harmonization is conducting round-robin testing to identify and eliminate procedural inconsistencies among labs. ISO/TC 229 has two task groups working to better understand *sustainability and societal impacts of nanotechnology*. The *applications of nanotechnology* are inherently global. It is important to ensure that the benefits of applications, such as energy efficiency, better pharmaceuticals, and environmental remediation, accrue to all segments of society. One advantage of nanotechnology is that *the barriers to entry are relatively low*, encouraging developing countries to get involved. Dr. Clancy concluded his presentation by challenging the NNI and its agencies to continue to incorporate international thinking into their activities.

Ethical, Legal, and Societal Implications

Barbara Herr Harthorn, University of California Santa Barbara

Prof. Herr Harthorn described how social scientists who study the ethical, legal, and societal implications (ELSI) of nanotechnology explore society's views on the benefits and potential risks. The National Science Foundation supports two Centers for Nanotechnology in Society (CNS-UCSB at University of California Santa Barbara and CNS-ASU at Arizona State University), which together provide the largest nanotechnology-related ELSI research and education infrastructure in the world. Prof. Herr Harthorn described five key themes of research on the societal implications of nanotechnology:

- Global R&D—Research performed in developing countries is rapidly improving in both quality and quantity. There is also a need for equitable development of nanotechnology in the global south.
- The Nanotechnology Workplace—Surveys have shown that industry often implements recommended environmental, health, and safety (EHS) practices, but disposal and waste management practices for ENMs and NEPs are not widespread. Larger companies generally have more sophisticated approaches, while small and medium enterprises have higher percentages of workers handling manufactured nanomaterials but less EHS infrastructure.
- Risk and Benefit Perception—As science and public understanding of nanotechnology co-evolve, it is important to iteratively survey the public and to understand that there is not one "public." Instead there are groups of stakeholders with different beliefs and values; CNS-UCSB research shows that risk communication should be tailored to each specific audience. Generally, publics in the United States still perceive more benefits than risks from nanotechnologies, but their opinions may change, and more high-quality information is needed.

- Public Engagement—The features of successful engagement activities are known in the academic community, but multistakeholder engagement is difficult. Prof. Herr Harthorn described the intensive outreach activities at CNS-ASU over a two-year period that had measurable societal impacts on the practices, activities, and knowledge of organizations.
- Governance—One model for anticipatory governance, also from CNS-ASU, has four key components: foresight, engagement, integration across fields, and "ensemble-ization" because nothing works in isolation. Successful governance is an iterative process that adapts based on evolving needs and information.

Prof. Herr Harthorn noted that the nanotechnology ELSI research program and community are well established because these issues are emphasized and supported by the NNI. She argued that it is vital to maintain this infrastructure to support future NNI activities.

Environmental, Health, and Safety Considerations

David Warheit, DuPont Haskell Global Centers for Health and Environmental Sciences

Dr. Warheit first summarized early research that demonstrated similar toxicity properties in nanoscale titanium dioxide and larger particles when surface area was taken into account. He emphasized that since the publication of that study, novel toxicity properties have not been demonstrated in ENMs when compared to effects demonstrated with fine particle toxicity.

The Nano Risk Framework[45] was developed to manage potential EHS effects across a product's life cycle. The Framework includes six iterative steps, and considerable emphasis is placed on profiling the properties, hazards, and exposure. To illustrate how this framework is used, Dr. Warheit described research on nanoscale titanium dioxide. He highlighted the importance of thoroughly characterizing the particles' properties, measuring dose response, examining response over time, and using controls in the study. The main finding was that biological response was commensurate with the particles' surface reactivity.

Dr. Warheit's research group has done multiple studies with the goal of reducing experiments in living organisms and transitioning to *in vitro* experiments. One study examined a variety of particles *in vivo* and *in vitro*. The results from the two systems were not consistent, meaning that *in vitro* studies are good for mechanistic studies but are still not sufficient for hazard screens. Dr. Warheit argued that more sophisticated *in vitro* systems are needed to better simulate biological systems.

Reliable, validated, and predictive high-throughput screening assays are still not available, and there is a paucity of reliable *in vivo* data, which is needed to establish a foundation for developing new tools. Dr. Warheit suggested building an *in vivo* database of five to ten representative ENM types. Using this database, *in vitro* and *in silico* results could be compared to those from *in vivo* findings. Additional needs include increased use of dose- and time-course studies; more complex experimental designs such as longer-term exposure/post-exposure periods, relevant doses, and dose metrics; and appropriate target cells that better simulate relevant exposure routes, as well as the development of standardized reference and benchmark nanomaterials.

---

[45] www.nanoriskframework.com

Breakout Sessions

Breakout sessions were held on five themes: EHS Considerations; Infrastructure Needs; Ethical, Legal, and Societal Implications; Commercializing Nanotechnology; and Technical Challenges. On the first day, participants were asked to answer several targeted questions.[46] The breakout sessions reconvened on the second day to review the goals and objectives from the 2011 NNI Strategic Plan. Participants were invited to provide input on potential changes in emphasis areas, new opportunities and challenges, and specific topics with significant potential for impact in the next three to five years.

Environmental, Health, and Safety Considerations

Co-Chairs: Richard Canady (ILSI Research Foundation), **Charles Geraci** (National Institute for Occupational Safety and Health), and **Thabet Tolaymat** (U.S. Environmental Protection Agency)

There is still great interest in nanotechnology-related EHS issues, as evidenced by the fact that over half of the workshop attendees participated in the two EHS breakout sessions. A diverse group of stakeholders provided input on barriers, gaps, and opportunities to further support EHS research on ENMs and NEPs.

The greatest impediment to progress in EHS research, as outlined by breakout session attendees, is the complex and multidisciplinary nature of nanotechnology. There are many types of ENMs with varying surface functionalities that will be exposed to different media throughout their life cycles. Transformations of ENMs at various life cycle stages and difficulties associated with measuring multiple ENM properties and NEP stability in realistic media add to the challenge of science-based risk assessment. Finally, progress in EHS research is predicated on communication and collaborations among researchers in many disciplines, including physical, chemical, biological, health, environmental, and social sciences.

Given the complexity of ENMs as well as EHS communications and collaboration challenges, the stakeholders identified a robust nanotechnology-related environmental, health, and safety (nanoEHS) informatics infrastructure as a requirement to relate ENM properties, exposure, and hazard knowledge sets for the various communities. Participants emphasized the following critical features for this infrastructure as it develops: (1) a compendium of existing methods, reference materials and consensus standards, and data organized in a coherent manner; (2) an ability to easily add such information as it becomes available; (3) transparent sharing of information; and (4) validation of methods and data. Attendees also called for increased emphasis in the following areas: sustainability; exposure and toxicity data that inform risk assessment of current or reasonably anticipated uses of nanotechnology; high-throughput screening tools; environmental fate and transport measurements and models; ENMs in food; dose metrics; and methods to distinguish ENMs from naturally occurring nanomaterials. The creation of a repository of well-characterized ENMs available for testing by researchers and for use in international interlaboratory studies was identified as a final high-priority research need.

Some breakout session attendees expressed concern that it is difficult to gauge progress toward NNI goals and objectives because the broad, long-ranging focus of the strategic plan is difficult to relate to specific near-term objectives. Stakeholders indicated that the NNI could better communicate progress

---

[46] Available at www.nano.gov/stakeholderworkshop.

by various means, such as a "dashboard" of progress for each objective in the plan and a stand-alone document containing detailed examples of NNI successes in EHS activities and best practices associated with the strategic plan. Finally, participants recommended that NNI agencies take action to make EHS a more critical part of their nanotechnology portfolios.

As a new opportunity, the participants recommended that the NNI agencies and the National Nanotechnology Coordination Office (NNCO) proactively interact with industry to learn about R&D and commercialization trends. This would enable the NNI agencies and industry to collaboratively identify EHS issues early in product development and to provide guidance on nanoEHS research. Further, attendees discussed the need for public–private partnerships for applied development of technology to support effective EHS implementation. Stakeholders also suggested that the NNI agencies better connect with regional, state, and local EHS activities and assist where appropriate in identifying and implementing best practices. On the international front, participants encouraged the NNI agencies to be more engaged in standards development organizations and to participate more in the OECD WPMN program of coordinated EHS research. Finally, the participants encouraged the Nanoscale Science, Engineering, and Technology Subcommittee to consider creating an NSI on high-throughput screening to support rapid identification and characterization of hazards and exposures.

Infrastructure Needs

Co-Chairs: Robert Rudnitsky (National Institute of Standards and Technology) and **Donald Tennant** (Cornell Nanoscale Science and Technology Facility)

The infrastructure needs breakout sessions were attended by representatives from government, national labs, and academia, including university education networks and user facilities. The topics addressed in the discussions fell into two distinct themes: physical infrastructure and formal and informal education.

One of the core concepts that shaped the discussion on physical infrastructure was the idea that nanotechnology R&D is accelerating and expanding. Therefore, participants noted, it is important to continually engage with users to ensure that their needs are met. Stakeholders urged that the funding for well-utilized shared facilities needs to be institutionalized to meet the long-term needs of the community. Rising costs of staff salaries, process materials, and safety measures due to inflation are often overlooked in flat funding planning. Further, capital investment is needed to increase flexibility, meet changing research needs, and extend the life of the highly invested facilities.

Stakeholders recognized that many startup companies rely on user facilities to develop their products. Given the critical role that these facilities play in research, development, and commercialization, breakout session attendees recommended that (1) facilities should be better equipped than those in start-up companies and small and medium enterprises; (2) NNI agencies with small business funding promote and seed the use of facilities to accelerate progress and improve the chance for successful commercialization; and (3) NNI facilities better engage with industry. Promotion of shared user facilities would be improved with an intelligent web-based service that informs and differentiates services among the various infrastructure options.

Shared user facilities not only provide a key technical service but also create a community of shared ideas by mixing researchers from different disciplines. However, participants noted several steps that could be taken to improve the efficacy and efficiency of user facilities. These include grants that allow smaller facilities to use the equipment replaced by larger facilities as well as the development of better metrology tools. Finally, some participants recommended the creation of an open facility or a distributed virtual facility for synthesizing materials to support the Materials Genome Initiative.

Education is a critical factor in the success of the NNI. Stakeholders argued that both formal and information education approaches need to be continued, supported, and expanded. The importance of informal education programs in helping the public understand the basic principles of nanoscience was noted. A well-informed public will be able to accurately weigh the opportunities of nanotechnology against any potential impacts. Attendees also suggested that the NNI publicize nanotechnology success stories. Finally, several participants recognized that exposure to nanotechnology concepts could ignite students' enthusiasm for science, technology, engineering, and mathematics (STEM) topic and careers.

Formal nanotechnology education is needed at multiple academic levels. In K–12 programs, nanotechnology-based curricula can be used to support student comprehension of crucial concepts from chemistry, physics, and biology. One participant further noted that associate-level, undergraduate, and post-graduate education should support the multidisciplinary nature of nanotechnology. There was particular enthusiasm in the group for educational approaches that extend beyond the traditional classroom. Possible alternatives include online courses, computer simulations of nanoscale phenomena, and remote access to nanoscience equipment.

Ethical, Legal, and Societal Implications

Co-Chairs: David Berube (North Carolina State University) and **Fred Kronz** (National Science Foundation)

Participants in the ELSI breakout session represented academia, government, industry, and nongovernmental organizations. The discussion was wide-ranging and addressed, among other topics, barriers and opportunities to engaging the public and supporting ELSI research.

Over the last ten years, the social science of nanotechnology has been established. Metrics documenting this transformation include the number of professional associations, the population of international scholars, the body of social science scholarship associated with nanotechnology, and the range of methods (descriptive, qualitative, and quantitative) used, including the use of mixed methods. For these reasons, stakeholders noted that the community is well-poised to address key ELSI issues associated with nanotechnology growth, including engagement, equity, governance, innovation, policy, risk perception and communication, and values. Some of the noteworthy successes have been numerous productive engagement exercises involving multiple stakeholder communities. Embedding social scientists within the laboratory affects views on a variety of social issues and the trajectory of nanotechnology research. Improving collaboration between laboratory and social scientists has co-shaped the understanding of socio-technical systems as they relate to nanotechnology. Breakout session attendees noted that these relationships need to be cultivated and enhanced as nanotechnology matures.

In the next three to five years, stakeholders envision a number of specific, pertinent challenges and requirements:

- Public exposure to risk messages has traditionally been managed by the mass media, but newer forms of digital media (such as blogs and news accumulators) have supplemented, and in some cases, replaced mass media.
- Deeper research studies on public perceptions of nanotechnology need to be conducted; in particular, scientists need to understand *why* members of the public perceive risk information the way they do. Further, phenomena such as "probability neglect" and "confirmation bias" need to be examined.
- Deeper research studies are also needed on experts' perceptions of the public (e.g., the public is not homogenous; public attitudes are context-specific; experts, while part of the public, may not represent public attitudes; and the public can be subject-matter experts).
- A high-priority challenge concerns being proactive, rather than reactive, to potential nanotechnology-related risk events.
- Another high-priority challenge is advancing innovation with research in emergent, salient, and exigent societal needs, defined in part by the public.

Participants highlighted the fact that institutionalized support for social science research is needed to meet the challenges above. This may be accomplished via a vision for future challenges and solutions, a greater number of experts, socio-technical infrastructure, and an increased capacity for public deliberation. Stakeholders recommended that the NNI agencies create and sustain opportunities for the public to participate in life cycle analysis. The inclusion of social scientists in broad impact assessment of overall NNI effectiveness was suggested; the roles of social scientists are multiple in nature—analysts, translators, integrators, facilitators, and colleagues.

Commercializing Nanotechnology

Co-Chairs: Michael Meador (National Aeronautics and Space Administration) and **Skip Rung** (Oregon Nanoscience and Microtechnologies Institute)

The focus of this session was on ways that NNI agencies can facilitate commercialization of nanotechnology-based discoveries. The breakout session was well attended by a broad spectrum of scientists, engineers, and business development professionals from the Federal Government; industry; regional, state and local partnerships; and academia.

Some "lessons learned" can be gleaned from successful models for commercialization of emerging technologies. Government agencies, universities, and industry are taking some innovative approaches in this area, including providing licenses to startup companies at minimal or no up-front cost and providing matching funds for third-party investment in successful Small Business Innovation Research (SBIR) and Small Business Technology Transfer Research (STTR) activities (e.g., the National Science Foundation's SBIR/STTR Supplemental Funding Program).[47]

Successful commercialization of nanotechnology requires strong interactions between technology innovators and end users. Stakeholders noted that NNI agencies could promote such interactions by incorporating them in review criteria for new and renewal grant proposals and including industrial scientists as members of proposal review panels.

---

[47] www.nsf.gov/eng/iip/sbir/Supplement

A greater awareness of promising nanotechnologies under development is a critical component to facilitate technology transfer and commercialization. Participants recommended that the NNI agencies and NNCO foster this exchange by providing a forum to publicize available technologies as well as industry "grand challenges" to focus nanotechnology R&D efforts.

Breakout session attendees highlighted the need for greater NNI agency participation and coordination in standards and specification activities to remove barriers to nanotechnology commercialization. It was noted that the development of harmonized standards is needed, both within the United States and internationally. Participants argued that reviews of existing specifications used by Federal agencies are needed to remove unneeded or outdated specifications that limit opportunities for insertion of new technologies. Based on the discussion points above, stakeholders noted that the following high-level concepts merit serious consideration going forward:

- *Opportunity Discovery.* The terms "commercializing research" and "technology transfer" do not adequately capture the importance and difficulty of market pull and customer traction to a new company or product line. Professional investors (including corporations) work to reduce not just technology risk, but also management-team, market, and financial risk. Participants suggested that NNI agencies implement strategies and set commercialization objectives (e.g., leveraged capital funding, jobs) and success metrics that will result in businesses that are attractive to private investors.
- *Corporate Engagement.* With a few exceptions (e.g., semiconductor and defense industries), industry engagement with NNI projects (sponsored research, corporate venture capital investments) seems sporadic and well below potential. Breakout session attendees recommended that NNI agencies engage with industry to discover what companies require in order to deploy their R&D funds.
- *Regional, State, and Local Partnership Funding.* States and regions are hungry for innovation-based economic development, and some are funding nanotechnology initiatives focused on commercialization. Participants suggested that NNI agencies look at this as a type of consortium opportunity with essential Federal and local early-stage funding and commercialization assistance components.
- *Regulatory Science.* Regulation protects the public but may also create formidable uncertainty and cost barriers, especially for startups and/or (initially) small businesses. Stakeholders noted that a scientific and future-oriented approach to harmonized and minimally intrusive regulation is needed.

Technical Challenges
Co-Chairs: Ali Shakouri (Purdue University) and **David Stepp** (U.S. Army Research Office)

The Technical Challenges breakout sessions were attended by nearly equal numbers of academic, industry, and government representatives and resulted in very productive and engaging discussions. Although the breakout sessions were framed differently each day, the discussions led to common key technical challenges and related suggestions.

Stakeholders acknowledged the significant progress and breadth of nanotechnology-related R&D activities as well as the general transition from passive nanoparticles to more complex structures and systems. However, participants identified concurrent scale-up with increased functionality as a remaining challenge. Application of nanotechnology in food and agriculture was broadly identified as an emerging opportunity area by the attendees. The group identified the most significant technical challenges facing the community as:

- The ability to make nanoparticles and structures with exquisite atomic-level control.
- The ability to fully characterize nanoparticles and nanostructures at the atomic level.
- The ability to model nanoparticles, structures, and systems at the atomic level.

With regard to the NNI agencies' R&D portfolio, the attendees identified the importance of identifying targets and focus areas that are unique to nanotechnology. They acknowledged the need for both individual and large-center support across the spectrum of fundamental to goal-oriented and applied nanotechnology research, as well as a unique opportunity to fund small interdisciplinary teams of 3–4 researchers. They articulated the necessity for big ideas or grand challenges to drive the overall community and help define the Initiative, while also allowing room for discovery. The importance of engaging new investigators in nanotechnology R&D was highlighted, especially in challenging budget times where established researchers may be more competitive. The attendees also emphasized the desire for more stakeholder engagement, including in workshops and webinars.

The participants discussed the challenges associated with developing meaningful assessment and raised questions regarding the quality and value of previous reviews. They recommended that NNI agencies pursue additional means of evaluation incorporating a dynamic exchange of information. They also recommended that reviews be aggressive in identifying successes and challenges.

The stakeholders expressed strongly the needs to clearly define the purpose and role of the NSIs and to clearly articulate the evaluation criteria for the establishment, review, and eventual transition of individual NSIs. They also suggested the inclusion of interdependent NSI goals and the evaluation of progress against those goals to further enhance cross-agency collaboration. It was recommended that all new NSIs define measurable goals and identify measures of success against which they would be evaluated in the initial white papers or proposals to the NSET Subcommittee. Suggested future topic areas included scalable manufacturing, health/food/nutrition, and nanotechnology for mobility.

Discussion included the importance of international collaboration on standards, communication, and leveraging expertise and unique resources. Recommended mechanisms included federally funded sabbaticals for U.S. researchers to work overseas and other forms of scientist exchange. Increased support for scientific meetings and conferences held in the United States was suggested as an effective way to facilitate productive interactions and communication among scientists from around the world. Travel restrictions and visas were mentioned as challenges.

Cross-Cutting Themes

Several recurrent themes emerged from the discussions across the breakout sessions. Participants repeatedly emphasized the need to further support collaborations across disciplinary, cultural, and sectoral boundaries. Multiple breakout sessions also noted the complementary needs to set clear metrics for success and to publicize successes when they are achieved. The need for international cooperation in the development of harmonized standards was also emphasized across the sessions. Finally, several groups requested additional support for forums where the nanotechnology community can engage across communities and with the Federal Government.

Appendix C: Overview of Former Program Component Areas (PCAs) and Comparison with Revised PCAs

Table C-1: Program Component Areas for Fiscal Years 2006–2014

No.	PCA Title	Description
1	Fundamental Nanoscale Phenomena and Processes	Discovery and development of fundamental knowledge pertaining to new phenomena in the physical, biological, and engineering sciences that occur at the nanoscale. Elucidation of scientific and engineering principles related to nanoscale structures, processes, and mechanisms.
2	Nanomaterials	Research aimed at the discovery of novel nanoscale and nanostructured materials and at a comprehensive understanding of the properties of nanomaterials (ranging across length scales, and including interface interactions). R&D leading to the ability to design and synthesize, in a controlled manner, nanostructured materials with targeted properties.
3	Nanoscale Devices and Systems	R&D that applies the principles of nanoscale science and engineering to create novel, or to improve existing, devices and systems. Includes the incorporation of nanoscale or nanostructured materials to achieve improved performance or new functionality. To meet this definition, the enabling science and technology must be at the nanoscale, but the systems and devices themselves are not restricted to that size.
4	Instrumentation Research, Metrology, and Standards for Nanotechnology	R&D pertaining to the tools needed to advance nanotechnology research and commercialization, including next-generation instrumentation for characterization, measurement, synthesis, and design of materials, structures, devices, and systems. Also includes R&D and other activities related to development of standards, including standards for nomenclature, materials characterization and testing, and manufacture.
5	Nanomanufacturing	R&D aimed at enabling scaled-up, reliable, and cost-effective manufacturing of nanoscale materials, structures, devices, and systems. Includes R&D and integration of ultra-miniaturized top-down processes and increasingly complex bottom-up or self-assembly processes.
6	Major Research Facilities and Instrumentation Acquisition	Establishment of user facilities, acquisition of major instrumentation, and other activities that develop, support, or enhance the Nation's scientific infrastructure for the conduct of nanoscale science, engineering, and technology R&D. Includes ongoing operation of user facilities and networks.
7*	Environment, Health, and Safety	Research primarily directed at understanding the environmental, health, and safety impacts of nanotechnology development and corresponding risk assessment, risk management, and methods for risk mitigation.
8*	Education and Societal Dimensions	Education-related activities such as development of materials for schools, undergraduate programs, technical training, and public communication, including outreach and engagement. Research directed at identifying and quantifying the broad implications of nanotechnology for society, including social, economic, workforce, educational, ethical, and legal implications.

* From 2004 – 2007, PCAs 7 and 8 were grouped as a single PCA called "Societal Dimensions."

Table C-2 presents a simple crosswalk between the former and new program component areas (PCAs) for continuity and historical reference. A few comments may help clarify the significance of the revisions.

Nanomaterials often has been a problematic PCA in that much research associated with novel nanomaterials and materials processing has been conducted at the fundamental research level. Moreover, this research may be conducted either within broader, basic research projects or as exploratory efforts associated with the production of novel nanomaterials or nanostructures and examination of their properties, but without specific applications in mind. In contrast, other work in this area is focused on R&D of nanomaterials and related processing, driven by specific applications or the achievement of specific properties. The new PCAs attempt to make a clearer separation between efforts that are fundamental and generic (foundational) and those that are applicative and specific.

Nanomanufacturing has proven to be exceptionally difficult to neatly categorize and clearly define for fiscal tracking. Research associated with processing and design technologies for microelectronic devices, for instance, is typically categorized and tracked with *Nanoscale Devices and Systems*. This delineation is both realistic and appropriate. Although it is possible and useful at times to identify R&D that facilitates processing and manufacturing, it appears preferable within PCAs to consider R&D foundational when generic and applicative when suitably so. Nanomanufacturing is and is expected to remain an extremely important part of the Initiative as evidenced by the establishment of a Nanotechnology Signature Initiative (NSI) focused on it. Nevertheless, with respect to the broader PCAs, it seems preferable to track processing and manufacturing efforts where they support broader projects and programs.

Finally, the *Education and Societal Dimensions* PCA has not been as useful as originally expected in showing either the magnitude or significance of efforts in these very important areas. Most research efforts have been associated with a very limited number of agencies and often within a subtextual part of the research thrust. Because PCAs are associated with funded R&D efforts, this PCA did not capture well the important related activities within the agencies that have not been part of R&D projects. It seems preferable, therefore, to report and track such efforts as they relate to established goals and objectives, whether primarily R&D or otherwise. As far as the R&D funding for such efforts is concerned, the expectation is that funding will be largely captured in the *Foundational Research* PCA.

Table C-2: Crosswalk between Former and Revised PCAs[48]

	2. Foundational Research	3. Nanotechnology-Enabled Applications, Devices, and Systems	4. Research Infrastructure and Instrumentation	5. Environment, Health, and Safety
1. Fundamental Nanoscale Phenomena and Processes	■			
2. Nanomaterials	■	■		
3. Nanoscale Devices and Systems		■		■
4. Instrumentation Research, Metrology, and Standards for Nanotechnology			■	
5. Nanomanufacturing	■	■	■	
6. Major Research Facilities and Instrumentation Acquisition			■	
7. Environment, Health, and Safety				■
8. Education and Societal Dimensions	■		■	■

KEY: ■ Correspondence between former and revised PCAs

[48] All activities specifically contributing to an NSI are now tracked under PCA 1: Nanotechnology Signature Initiatives. For example, a project that was previously listed under PCA 1: Fundamental Nanoscale Phenomena and Processes could potentially be categorized under PCA 1: Nanotechnology Signature Initiatives (if the scope of the project falls under an NSI) or PCA 2: Foundational Research (if the scope does not fall under an NSI) in the new system.

Appendix D. Abbreviations and Acronyms

the Act	The 21st Century Nanotechnology Research and Development Act of 2003
ARS	Agricultural Research Service (USDA)
ATSDR	Agency for Toxic Substances and Disease Registry (DHHS)
BIS	Bureau of Industry and Security (DOC)
BRAIN Initiative	Brain Research through Advancing Innovative Neurotechnologies Initiative
CNST	Center for Nanoscale Science and Technology (DOC/NIST)
CoT	Committee on Technology (NSTC)
CNS-ASU	Center for Nanotechnology in Society at Arizona State University
CNS-UCSB	Center for Nanotechnology in Society at University of California Santa Barbara
CPSC	Consumer Product Safety Commission
CSREES	Cooperative State, Research, Education, and Extension Service (now USDA/NIFA)
DHS	Department of Homeland Security
DHHS	Department of Health and Human Services
DOC	Department of Commerce
DOD	Department of Defense
DOE	Department of Energy
DOEd	Department of Education
DOI	Department of the Interior
DOJ	Department of Justice
DOL	Department of Labor
DOS	Department of State
DOT	Department of Transportation
DOTreas	Department of the Treasury
EDA	Economic Development Administration (DOC)
EHS	environment(al), health, and safety
ELSI	ethical, legal, and societal implications (of nanotechnology)
ENM	engineered nanomaterial
EOP	Executive Office of the President
EPA	Environmental Protection Agency
ETIPC	Emerging Technologies Interagency Policy Coordination Committee
FDA	Food and Drug Administration (DHHS)
FHWA	Federal Highway Administration (DOT)
FS	Forest Service (USDA)
GIN	Global Issues in Nanotechnology (former NSET working group)
IC	Intelligence Community
IEC	International Electrotechnical Commission
ISO	International Organization for Standardization
LED	light-emitting diode
MGI	Materials Genome Initiative
nanoEHS	nanotechnology-related environment(al), health, and safety
NASA	National Aeronautics and Space Administration
NCI	National Cancer Institute (DHHS/NIH)
NCL	Nanotechnology Characterization Laboratory (DHHS/NIH/NCI)
NCNR	NIST Center for Neutron Research (DOC/NIST)
NEHI	Nanotechnology Environmental and Health Implications Working Group (NSET)

NEP	Nanotechnology-enabled product
NIEHS	National Institute of Environmental Health Sciences (DHHS/NIH)
NIFA	National Institute of Food and Agriculture (USDA)
NIH	National Institutes of Health (DHHS)
NIJ	National Institute of Justice (DOJ)
NILI	Nanomanufacturing, Industry Liaison, and Innovation Working Group (NSET)
NIOSH	National Institute for Occupational Safety and Health (DHHS)
NIST	National Institute of Standards and Technology (DOC)
NKI	Nanotechnology Knowledge Infrastructure (NSI)
NNAP	National Nanotechnology Advisory Panel (PCAST)
NNCO	National Nanotechnology Coordination Office
NNI	National Nanotechnology Initiative
NNIN	National Nanotechnology Infrastructure Network
NRC	Nuclear Regulatory Commission
NRC/NA	National Research Council of the National Academies
NRI	Nanoelectronics Research Initiative
NRO	National Reconnaissance Office (IC)
NSET	Nanoscale Science, Engineering, and Technology Subcommittee of the NSTC Committee on Technology
NSF	National Science Foundation
NSI	Nanotechnology Signature Initiative
NSRC	Nanoscale Science Research Centers (DOE program)
NSTC	National Science and Technology Council
NTRC	Nanotechnology Research Center (DHHS/NIOSH)
ODNI	Office of the Director of National Intelligence (IC)
OECD	Organisation for Economic Co-operation and Development
OMB	Office of Management and Budget (Executive Office of the President)
OSHA	Occupational Safety and Health Administration (DOL)
OSTP	Office of Science and Technology Policy (EOP)
PCA	Program Component Area
PCAST	President's Council of Advisors on Science and Technology
R&D	research and development
RSL	regional, state, and local organizations
SAICM	Strategic Approach to International Chemical Management
SBIR	Small Business Innovation Research program
SciENcv	Science Experts Network Curriculum Vitae
STAR METRICS™	Science and Technology for America's Reinvestment: Measuring the Effect of Research on Innovation, Competitiveness and Science
STEM	science, technology, engineering, and mathematics
STTR	Small Business Technology Transfer research program
TC 229	Technical Committee 229 (ISO)
USITC	U.S. International Trade Commission
USPTO	U.S. Patent and Trademark Office (DOC)
USDA	U.S. Department of Agriculture
USGS	U.S. Geological Survey (DOI)
WPMN	Working Party on Manufactured Nanomaterials (OECD)
WPN	Working Party on Nanotechnology (OECD)